Know Yourself & LIVE FREE

BRIAN M. TYSDAL

 FriesenPress

One Printers Way
Altona, MB R0G 0B0
Canada

www.friesenpress.com

Copyright © 2025 by Brian M. Tysdal
First Edition — 2025

Cover illustration by Britney Burghardt — britney43110@gmail.com

All rights reserved.

No part of this publication may be reproduced in any form, or by any means, electronic or mechanical, including photocopying, recording, or any information browsing, storage, or retrieval system, without permission in writing from FriesenPress.

ISBN
978-1-03-832867-0 (Hardcover)
978-1-03-832866-3 (Paperback)
978-1-03-832868-7 (eBook)

1. RELIGION, CHRISTIAN LIVING, SPIRITUAL GROWTH

Distributed to the trade by The Ingram Book Company

New Living Translation: "Scripture quotations marked *NLT* are taken from the *Holy Bible*, New Living Translation, copyright © 1996, 2004, 2015 by Tyndale House Foundation. Used by permission of Tyndale House Publishers, Carol Stream, Illinois 60188. All rights reserved."

New International Version: "Scripture quotations taken from The Holy Bible, New International Version® NIV®.Copyright © 1973, 1978, 2011 by Biblica, Inc.™ Used by permission. All rights reserved worldwide."

Amplified Bible: "Scripture quotations taken from *The Amplified Bible*. Copyright © 1954, 1958, 1962, 1965, 1987 by The Lockman Foundation. All rights reserved. Used by permission. (www.Lockman.org)."

The Passion Translation: "Scripture quotations marked TPT are from The Passion Translation®.Copyright © 2017 by Broad Street Publishing® Group, LLC. Used by permission. All rights reserved. thePassionTranslation.com."

New American Standard Bible: "Scripture quotations taken from the (NASB®) New American Standard Bible®,Copyright © 1960, 1971, 1977, 1995, 2020 by The Lockman Foundation. Used by permission. All rights reserved. lockman.org."

"Thank You"

To my wife who has willingly and joyfully wed her life to mine. I love you and am amazed that you chose me and that you choose me still. Thank you for encouraging me to step out to share my thoughts with the world.

Book Endorsements

"Every human being has complicated identities but each disciple of Jesus has a foundational personal and theological identity—a brand new identity in Christ! Brian Tysdal, from his personal journey, his years of ministry experience and the study of Scripture provides the WHY and HOW to be truly Spirit-led and experience true freedom! In light of what God has accomplished in Christ, Brian passionately invites all of us to embrace whole-life transformation and lavishly taste spiritual victory right here and right now!"

>Rev. Dr. T.V. Thomas
>Chairman, Lausanne Global Diaspora Network

"Are you a weary follower of Jesus, exhausted from trying to penetrate your hardened heart with inadequate tools? Brian Tysdal reminds us that there is another way. The true transformation of the soul is a ministry of hope and consolation rooted in an identity formed in Christ. Brian speaks the language of the heart truly and sincerely, and he invites us to watch as the Holy Spirit 'testifies with our spirit that we are God's children... heirs of God and co-heirs with Christ.' (Romans 8:16-17). Brian reminds us that knowledge of God is not primarily about information, it is about relationship, a relationship that is life-giving and liberating."

>The Rev. Canon Dr. Dean Pinter
>Canon Theologian
>Cathedral Church of the Advent

"*Know Yourself and Live Free* is a profound and transformative journey into self-discovery through the lens of faith. With deep theological insights and heartfelt personal reflections, my friend, Brian Tysdal, masterfully unpacks what it means to live in the freedom of our God-given identity. This book is a must-read for anyone seeking clarity in their spiritual walk, struggling with self-worth, or yearning for a deeper connection with God. It challenges, encourages, and ultimately leads readers toward a liberating understanding of who they truly are in Christ."

    Al Fedorak
    Retired teacher, pastor, and denominational leader

"In *Know Yourself and Live Free,* Brian Tysdal has written a field guide for Christian living! Brian helps us understand what Christian identity is and why our identity in Christ is so important for authentic Christian living. He brings clarity to what the Bible says about the soul and the spirit and the role they play in shaping our identity and then guides us through a number of scriptural concepts like grace, forgiveness, humility, surrender, holiness and abiding in Christ. He drills down into the biblical meaning of these concepts, and then uses personal anecdotes and down-to-earth illustrations to help us understand and live out these concepts by the enabling power of the Holy Spirit.

    Wes Mills
    President, Apostolic Church of Pentecost

"Brian Tysdal, pastor, shepherd, teacher and friend, compellingly invites each soul that reads *Know Yourself and Live Free* to a life surrendered to the Spirit of God in such a way that it brings clarity to our identity and freedom to live in obedience to the 'audaciously extravagant love of God." Brian is not only writing

about this journey—he is living it. Join this trusted guide as he champions your freedom!"
>Linda Kasdorf, MSW
>ThinkLife Empowerment Company

"In an age and world where we are constantly offered a compendium of bankrupt options upon which to ground our identities—gender, ethnicity, and political stripe just to name a few—Brian Tysdal, in an approachable and persuasive style, reminds the searching Christian that the ground of their identity, just like the ground of their salvation, is none other than Jesus!"
>Rev. Dr. Bernie Van De Walle
>Midwest District Superintendent
>Christian and Missionary Alliance Canada

"*Know Yourself and Live Free*, is an incredible gift to get clarity about questions of identity: Who is God? Who am I? Who has God made me to be? Brian authors a clear and compelling invitation to keep wrestling with these questions. His is an encouraging voice on the journey!"
>Glenn Petersen
>Senior Director of Church Planting
>Evangelical Covenant Church

"In *Know Yourself and Live Free*, Tysdal addresses the age old and most important questions many of us have in our lives; "Who am I?", "What is my identity?", in a way I have not seen before. His book is a must read for all who have asked these questions, for people of faith, and for those searching for meaning and faith in their own lives."
>Wayne L. Bernakevitch KC (King's Council)

Introduction

I REMEMBER MANY YEARS ago, as a little kid, going to church and having my routine. I would enter through the back door of the building and then go down the stairs to the basement and greet the people as I walked by. I would then go up the stairs to the main floor and do the same thing: I would greet everyone that was around me as I walked to the main level entrance.

I felt a visceral joy bubbling in me that I expressed with phrases like this: "Good morning! How are you today?" My enthusiasm was genuine because I wanted to connect with the people there and share a bit of that joy as I was able.

Now, I know as well as anyone that my memory of these exploits are probably a bit fuzzy, but as I remember it, it's true. It was an authentic desire within me to try and help others to feel like they belonged, and I too wanted to feel like I belonged in and among all those people who had gathered to worship.

I think this is a deeply rooted impulse that's embedded in each and every human being... ... an inescapable drive to be a part of something that helps you to know that you fit. And as you continue to walk this out in your life, you begin to realize that there is more going on than simply wanting to fit in with others; there grows in you a sense that you're also trying to get clearer understanding about who you are. You begin to ask questions about yourself: "Why do I respond the way I do to people?", "What is it that gives me a sense of purpose and meaning?", "Why do I feel the things I feel?" And really, at the end of the day you ask yourself, "Who am I?"

I think this has been a theme in my life, really. I have been on a multi-decade journey of self-discovery. Plato once said, "The unexamined life is not worth living." I think he was onto something here... to live by simply being reactive to your surroundings, is to avoid allowing yourself to sit and entertain the thoughts that can only arise when you slow down enough to let those deep-down feelings and memories bubble to the surface of your mind. It's then that you begin to get some insight into a panorama of images and ideas that coalesce into a sense of wholeness. In this case, it's an emerging picture of who you are.

It's messy to be sure. We are a combination of hurts, traumas, victories, joys, and everything in between. We have been created in the image of God, and that image remains as a foundation for all of the data, detritus, and delight of a life lived. At the end of the day, we *are*. Maybe that in itself, that we *are*, is a reflection of our image bearing of the God who calls Himself "I AM." I'm not saying that our image bearing is an indication of innate deity within us, but more that since we experience the wrestling of trying to understand the reality of our identity, we are expressing something that's more of a reflex, a response, to the One who has made us like Him.

For better or worse, no, for better *and* worse, we are the composite of a myriad of experiences. I remember the title of a book by James Sire that I used to teach for a worldview class at my beloved Eston College many, many years ago. The title of the book was *Universe Next Door*, and it's such an apt description of a human being. We are so complex; built so wonderfully and fearfully, that to sit beside another person is to literally sit beside an amalgamation of experiences that has created an entire universe distinct from my own. Unbelievable!

I want so badly to honour the uniqueness of each universe that I have the privilege to walk beside; to greet; to share a coffee; to incite an argument; to offer a needed shoulder to cry on; to join in a ridiculous song; to listen to another's journey; to glean insight; to hug; to fight; to fear, and to love. We are messy universes, to be sure. But, oh man, we are something to behold!

When I attained a slightly more advanced age, I had the privilege of writing my thesis for a master's degree in Religion, Culture, and Ethics from Trinity Western University, in Langley, British Columbia. I was looking at it the other day, and the title of it reminded me of a larger picture of the journey of my life. The title of my thesis was "In Search of Self…" This reminded me that searching for identity matters to me. It's the expression of the little boy who walked around his church greeting people on Sunday morning, and the young man who continued the search into his early thirties by examining texts from people who have been on this same search for centuries. And now, in my mid-fifties, I see in our day and age that identity is being redefined with an unprecedented pace and, sometimes, with a fierce and reckless abandon. It tells me that this is not only still a relevant issue, but it might just be a *defining* issue for us today.

And I kind of think that it's important to you too… so I'm really glad you're here.

I'd like to invite you on a bit of a journey of self-discovery. You need to know that I'm approaching this adventure from the perspective of one who is a disciple of Jesus Christ, holding to the idea that our identities have been crafted by the God of the Bible and that He's actively involved in not only creating the foundation of who we are, but is also creatively revealing to us an ongoing and dynamic montage of self-identity. We are literally masterpieces being painted in real time, all the time.

I would also like to tell you the method that I used in crafting this book. I have intentionally chosen to interact with Scripture only. I'm not using references from any other authors, and my own experiences and ongoing journey with God and the Bible, are my primary sources. If it seems as though this book would have benefitted from others' thoughts, part of me would say

"I agree," but I simply felt that my approach this time was to be very, very basic. So... with all that said...

If you're ready, then I say, "Let's go!"

CHAPTER 1

Setting the Stage

"If I do what I don't want to do, I am not really the one doing wrong: it is sin in me that does it" (Romans 7:20 NLT).

THIS MAY STRIKE YOU as kind of a depressing way to start off. But when I read this passage I am filled with excitement! Why? Because I know that we all struggle with sin, and its effects are real and sometimes profoundly impactful, and I know that when we begin to see a way toward freedom, it feels incredibly hope filled. When we begin to put pieces together in our lives, we see an emerging picture, and the picture that God is painting in and through us is beautiful. But that beautiful image is often clouded and difficult for us to see.

Even though I'm a child of God, I still experience real pain when I sin... it hurts! And it hurts enough that it can consume my thoughts and those thoughts can lead toward pretty dark places. There is real pain, and along with that pain is a feeling that I am doing something that is in direct opposition to something embedded deep inside of me. It feels like a betrayal. Somehow we all experience this emotion when we don't live according to the ideas and principles established by God. When I say I feel like my sinful actions elicit a sense of betrayal, I mean that it seems like I'm living in a way that's not really being true to what is right, but even more than that. When I do things, think things, or feel things that are not in alignment with my Holy heavenly Father, I feel like I'm somehow living as an imposter, like I'm operating in opposition to who I am, or at least to who I think I should be. I feel hypocritical.

Did you know that early actors in the Greek world were called *hypokrites* (pronounced hip-oh-crit-TAYS)? A stage actor would have been called a hypokrites because they were pretending to be someone they really weren't. They would sing, speak, and act a certain personality, but in real life they were someone else entirely. In fact, the actual meaning of *hypokrites* (English: hypocrite) is "an interpreter from underneath." It sounds strange until you realize that very early 1st century B.C. actors wore masks when they performed. And so a *hypokrites* was someone who interprets some aspect of life from underneath a mask.

That's what I can feel like when I'm living in some kind of sin while still calling myself a Christian and holding to a genuine faith in Jesus. On the outside I'm portraying what looks like a solid relationship with God, but on the inside, I'm struggling with this battle between holiness and sinfulness. I'm living as a hypocrite, an actor. I have my mask on the outside, and on the inside I'm filled with questions and doubts about who I really am.

At least that's what it feels like, and I'm sure that every person who finds themselves in relationship with Jesus Christ has experienced this kind of internal wrestling. That's the primary reason why I'm writing this book because I don't think we have a clear sense of who Jesus has made us to be and what His opinion of us really is. More than that... I don't think we understand what

His declaration about us really is! It's far more powerful than we imagine. And it's something we need to learn and absorb so we can experience the reality of the transformation of Jesus' life in us and live free. But we need to start by building a picture of this so we can unravel it and see through the tangled mess inside of ourselves. And so in order to see things more clearly, we need to look at the apostle Paul and what he wrote in Romans 7:20.

You Are Not What You Do

I love the apostle Paul. He's so open and honest about his journey of faith that it makes me feel like maybe I'm not the only one who's screwed up as I try to work out this crazy life with Jesus.

I think in the greater context of life, when I compare myself to the world around me, I think I know very few things. And I find that the older I get, I want to gain knowledge about even fewer things. But along with that desire to filter out much of the data of life, I get a sense of wanting to know those fewer things very deeply. It's like I'm searching for bedrock, that place where no matter what waves crash in, the thing I'm standing on is simply not going to move. It's a great feeling to find those things, especially when the heat is on in life. This is what Paul offers in the passage in Romans 7:20; it's a bridge to a new understanding that unearths some bedrock to help us begin to stand and understand who we really are.

We often associate *what we do* with *who we are*. Isn't that true? Imagine yourself at a wedding banquet, and people are milling about. You're filling your glass with punch and someone you don't know comes up beside you. You don't know them, but you're wanting to be friendly, so you introduce yourself and then, invariably, the next thing you ask is "so, what do you do?" Absolutely nothing wrong with asking that question! But if you take some time to examine your life, you begin to realize that we associate our identity so very deeply with what we do.

That's not to say that our choices and actions don't matter because they really do. It matters to God as well. Faith... that thing that's the essential link between us and Jesus, is talked about in James 2:17 NASB, where the brother of Jesus writes: "...faith, if it has no works, is dead, being by itself."

Faith. That relational linchpin that connects us to our life source has no life within it if it doesn't lead to action. The kind of faith that comes from God will produce the fruit of actions that reflect God. The actions don't produce faith but instead arise from it. We often get this mixed up and can get confused because these two things, faith and works, are so closely associated in our minds. But God doesn't seem to be afraid to make these close associations between things that might lead people astray if they misunderstand. He seems pretty comfortable taking these risks. What we read in James 2:17 is one of those examples.

This passage seems to say that if our actions aren't in alignment with our faith, then that isn't the kind of faith that God had in mind for His children. Faith and actions become *very* close. In fact they become so close that we can reverse the order of priority. Instead of faith being the first and primary element, we can make the actions the first and primary element. When we do this, we make our actions or our *works* the foundation that now no longer proves the existence of faith, but instead those actions become the foundation upon which faith is built. We have then bought into a works-oriented faith that requires us to earn a relationship with Jesus through what we do. When we get to this stage, we run into all kinds of trouble understanding our true identity because we now think that what we do is the foundation of who we are... even in Jesus.

By the way, Satan loves it when the children of God buy into the idea that we need to work hard in order to earn our salvation or relationship with Jesus, because He knows full well that it's an empty cistern with no water to satisfy. We will work ourselves literally to death in this way of living for Jesus.

We Love Control

One of the reasons that we are so attracted to this way of living out our faith is because we really love to control things in our lives. Sin, by its very nature, creates within us a desire for independence. We love the idea of Jesus as our Saviour, so after this life is done, we then can experience freedom with Him in the next life. But Jesus as Saviour becomes a problem for people who want to get things done now. We have agendas and limited time. We have things to do for others, and even Jesus, and when He tries to step in and be the captain of our ship, we get frustrated because someone other than us is running the show! When it comes to Jesus being our *Lord*, where He is now the One who tells us how we are to live and how we are to understand ourselves, we have some trouble.

It says in 1 Corinthians 6:19–20 "...you are not your own... you have been bought with a price..." Our life in Jesus is now *his*. It's not ours any longer but we often still try to make it our own. We do this by exerting control in our lives. And one prominent way we do that is by making faith about our actions instead of starting from the place of trust and following what the Lord tells us.

One of the most famous documents in human history is the Declaration of Independence of the United States. This is a clear statement of the newly established Union declaring their separation from Great Britain in order to attain their own identity. What Jesus wants from us is that we would proclaim our Declaration of *De*pendence and that we would find our identity in Him and not separately from Him. But we find ourselves struggling to grasp and consistently live out this high calling, just like the apostle Paul.

This love of control in us tempts us to try to manipulate our lives under our own self-created mandates. We begin to think that in order to achieve this, we then need a game plan, and that game plan includes things that we can control. Generally speaking, we can control what we *do*, our actions. If we invest enough time and energy into this way of living, what happens over time is that we crowd out other things that might be in the way of accomplishing our goals. If the goal is to live for Jesus, and living for Jesus means that we do things, and in order to do things well we need to control our circumstances, then we marshal our resources (time, talent, treasure, etc.) to accomplish this task. What this boils down to is living a Christian life for Jesus by controlling everything around us so we can accomplish much for Him. This touches so many areas of our lives that we lose sight of the fact that we have created an environment that becomes overwhelmingly saturated with this idea that if our lives are to have meaning, then they need to be very *productive*. Action becomes the defining characteristic of who we are.

Did you pay attention to that last line? What we do becomes who we think we are.

Undoing the Lie

This brings us back to what Paul is saying in Romans 7:20. Let's hear it again: *"If I do what I don't want to do, I am not really the one doing wrong: it is sin in me that does it."*

Paul is making an incredibly important distinction here. He's saying that if he does something wrong or sinful, then it isn't he that is doing it! *What do you mean, Paul, that it isn't you doing it? Of course it's you doing it because you did it!*

But Paul is teaching us something here that God revealed to him about his identity.

I'm going to say it again: there is a distinction being made here about identity... about who Paul *really* is, and it isn't based on his actions.

The lie that we often live into, or build up so greatly that we can only see through its lenses, is that we are what we do. Even if we do something wrong, then I need to take responsibility for those actions, and more so, we believe that what we did is evidence of who I am. The flip side of this same coin is to think that if I do something good, then I must receive accolades for my excellence, and along with this is that my praised actions also serve as evidence of who I am. Identity based on actions. Both views are fraught with danger. And this takes us even further into the nuances of identity, because God would agree that there are consequences for actions to be sure. When Ananias and Sapphira told a lie about their finances in Acts 5, they paid for their actions with their lives! What we do does matter. But I want you to know that this passage says nothing about the *identity* of Ananias and Sapphira. They paid a price for their actions, but their actions said nothing about who they are.

Go back to Paul. He said that he committed an action that was sinful. It was something that he didn't want to do, but he did it anyway. Did he then question his identity in Jesus? Was his identity based on what he did? It would seem not because he said that it was no longer he that did it but sin in him. Did he still feel the consequence of his actions? You bet he did! In verse 24 he calls himself "wretched." The Greek word Paul uses here is *talaiporos*, which comes from *talao*, "to bear or undergo" and *poros*, "a callous." What Paul is saying here is that his sinful action has caused him to feel miserable and distressed; he's distressed from continued strain which left callouses on his heart, leading to deep misery. The effects of his sin had caused him hardship in his heart, and these effects were severe.

Do you think Paul understands that his choice to sin has consequences? Most certainly yes! But does he think that his actions say something about his true identity? Not on your life. He makes it clear that it is not "I" that does it. His identity is found somewhere else. He has been given an identity that is somehow distinct from his actions in this case. He has found his unmovable foundation that proves itself stable even when the waves of sinful pain wash over him. Even when those waves of sinful pain come from within him! It's kind of hard to wrap your head around, but Paul sees his identity in Jesus as something that rises above sin and sinful actions, in very real ways.

Paul even uses a positive example to further his views of identity. He writes in 2 Corinthians 10:17-18 NIV: "Let the one who boasts boast in the Lord. For it is not the one who commends himself who is approved, but the one whom the Lord commends." What Paul is saying here is that even if he does something well, or even amazing, it's not for him to take credit for himself; that belongs to Jesus. Paul is not found or identified in himself or his own actions, but in Jesus alone. His whole life... everything that makes Paul truly Paul, that is to say *his identity*, is found in Jesus Christ. The emphasis of this goes to extreme lengths when Paul says in Romans 14:8 NIV, "If we live, we live for the Lord, and if we die, we die for the Lord. So then, whether we live or die, we are the Lord's."

For Paul, the only way he can understand his identity is through the lens of Jesus Christ. His own actions must be understood through this lens... even when he does something sinful, though there are consequences, they don't *define him*. Only Jesus does that.

This is the essence of what we are trying to understand here... that we've been given an identity that's so free it confounds all our attempts to limit it to our actions or our own control. As I write this, it sounds like freedom, but for some strange reason, it also feels scary. Freedom that knows no bounds confounds my ability to fully understand it, and those areas of uncharted territory require faith and trust that stretch me to my limits and beyond.

I'm reminded of how the Lord brought this home for me again through a time of personal prayer just the other day.

I'd been struggling for some time regarding my leadership of a ministry called Deeper Life. I was led to read about God's powerful moving in the book of Habakkuk. In this book it describes how God is promising to do amazing works among the people and the nations, in order to bring cleansing and righteousness to the land. But Habakkuk is frustrated because all he sees in his present circumstances is injustice and people who have abandoned righteousness. And he sees this everywhere around him! He cried out to the Lord about this, and God's response is this: "Wait and see."

Habakkuk was frustrated because he wasn't seeing the action of God to do what He said He would do. Habakkuk wanted results not just promises.

What Habakkuk didn't realize, however, was that he was setting himself up as judge over God. He felt that since God made a promise to do something, then it just makes sense that it should happen sooner rather than later. But God said, "Wait".

I had trouble seeing how this was relevant to my circumstances as the leader of Deeper Life Ministries, but then the Lord revealed something about me... This is what He said to me, "Brian, your pride hinders you."

I'd been given the vision for this ministry a number of years before. I'd been the one who had carried the burden of birthing it and carrying it forward. I'd felt a confidence in my leadership, but that had changed as more and more people got involved.

Among the many who were serving directly and indirectly in ministry, I felt that my influence had diminished. My voice was no longer the singular voice of direction but now one among many. Through all of this I began to operate with increased doubt and insecurity. Instead of serving the Lord and doing what He commanded, I was serving myself and trying to re-establish my influence. It became about my identity.

Along the way, what became more and more important was *what* was being done. I felt anxious if I didn't make decisions that put things in motion, and this was important, because if I was charting a course of action, then people could follow what I was saying. My relationship with people in this ministry became defined through my decisions and actions. Slowly and subtly, this became the foundation of my engagement with ministry and with those involved in it. Does that sound familiar?

The Lord saw all of this and summarized my convoluted journey by saying that pride had captured me. But do you know what He said to me after He identified my sin problem? He said "Faith reveals." And my response was, "*What?*" That didn't seem to make any sense at all to me. So I waited a bit, and things got clearer...

I was looking for answers to overcome my frustration and feeling of loss of leadership and influence. I was guilty of exerting increased control in order to gain what I felt I was losing. It became about me, though it was all cloaked in the garments of Christian service. Make no mistake, it had become about me, and I was operating as a hypocrite. I had on my external mask of Christian service and obedience all the while I was experiencing a blood-soaked battle between my soul and my spirit.

In my search for answers I had wandered away, and now the Lord was working to get me back on track. Instead of me operating out of an identity that was primarily based on myself and actions I could control, He was calling me to get into alignment with Him, which is all about faith and relationship. He was calling me to get my eyes back on Him. Please note that He was still wanting to provide answers: He said "Faith *reveals.*" He was going to reveal things to me that I needed in order to live out the identity that He had given to me in Him. This would include the things needed to lead ministry in an honouring way and would also allow me to walk in the fullness of Him as I kept my eyes on Him and not on myself. He would reveal what is needed when I needed it.

But I needed to give up my selfish actions and attempts to control. I needed to hear the same thing Habakkuk heard..."Wait."

When my flesh (worldly thinking or desires) is the thing that's driving me, there's very little that I will allow to get in the way of accomplishing the things that make sense to me. This is true even if what I'm operating in is killing me from the inside out. That's sin! That's exactly what sin does. It's so sneaky and deceptive, and our souls still wrestle in this way, even as saved sons and daughters in Christ.

In order to live in freedom, in order to live in the fullness of our identity given to us by Jesus, we need to understand not just who we are but also who we *aren't*. Our truest identity is not found in our best thoughts, actions, or intents, as good as they may seem. No. Our truest identity begins from the foundation of Jesus Christ and what He has done for us. Hear that again: our identity is not founded on what we do (physical actions/thoughts/choices/desires), but on what Jesus has done for us. And He has not just saved us; He has literally made us *new creations.*

I say He hasn't just saved us on purpose because we have adopted a view of salvation as something like fire insurance, the ticket that will allow us to get on the bus for heaven and avoid the one going to hell. This kind of view of salvation has one critically important aspect to it, everything about it remains distant, or external, from me. I may be holding the ticket with my name on it, but I'm still holding a ticket that is separate from me. No, this is not the kind of salvation that Jesus has given to me.

What he has given to me is not external from me, but instead has *transformed me from the inside*. When I said "yes" to Jesus as my Saviour, I said yes to becoming a brand new man. Not refurbished, not touched up, not just a couple of new parts in the old machine, but *brand new*. That is exactly how God sees His children... as brand new!

"But Brian," you may be asking, "How is it possible that you are a literally brand new person when you still say, do, think, and feel things that are sinful?"

My response to that would be this: "Because the Lord has given to me a new identity that is real but not comprehensive. What I mean is that the fullness of God in Jesus has been given to me and resides in my *spirit*. But my soul and body are still wrestling with sin. I have been *justified* in my spirit, but my soul and body are still in the process of becoming holy or *sanctified*."

Understanding God's view of this is of paramount importance. He says to those who have given their lives to Jesus that to Him, their *identity* is now fully found in Jesus and all that He provides. You, according to God, are now holy. Righteous. Set apart. Royalty. Overcomer. More than conqueror. And on and on and on. *This is now who you are.* And all of this resides in your spirit which has been fully renewed to its original state. But your soul (thinking, emotion, and will) is still wrestling with the effects of sin that are devastatingly powerful. And on top of that truth, it is through your soul that you live your daily life here on earth. All of your thoughts. All of your feelings. All of your choices. *All of your experiences, and your awareness of those experiences, take place in and through your soul.* Do you begin to see just how important it is to have your true identity revealed to you? If every aspect of your processing power (mind, emotion, and will) is blinded to your new identity in your spirit, then what we need is for someone to teach us and lead us *into* this new identity and all the benefits that come with it. Thankfully, that's exactly what

God is teaching us through His revealing Holy Spirit and Bible. And thankfully, He is absolutely committed to this task because He loves the idea of His children actually living in freedom!

Good words maybe, but how are we supposed to understand that in a way that really makes sense? We're going to explore that more as we look at the way in which God made us. He's given to us souls and spirits, and their function is very different. One is where we operate from (soul), and one is the foundation of our identity (spirit). Both are integral to our make-up and both have immense impact on how we understand who we are.

CHAPTER 2:

What Is the Soul?

IN CHAPTER 1 WE saw the passage in Romans 7:20 as important to begin our understanding that our identity is maybe not exactly what we imagined. Paul took note that when he did something that he knew was wrong, it wasn't *he* that did it, but instead it was sin in him that did it. This is just the beginning of seeing that somehow Paul's identity was not necessarily tied to his actions and also, at least in his own understanding, there was some kind of separation, distinction, or division within him.

Paul knew that his true identity was distinct from what caused him to act in a way that he knew was wrong. So what on earth could that mean? How do we understand this? Is there something in the Bible that would help us to see our identity in a way that really makes sense and would help us to live in real and experienced freedom?

The Bible tells us something very important about the different parts that make us human beings. In Hebrews 4:12 NASB it says, "For the word of God is living and active and sharper than any two-edged sword, and piercing as far as the division of soul and spirit, of both joints and marrow, and able to judge the thoughts and intentions of the heart."

Obviously, we know that as human beings we have physical bodies. But did you know that you have two immaterial parts? You have both a *soul* and a *spirit*, and they serve different functions. In fact they serve *very* different and important functions. So important, that it's within these two differing aspects of our make-up that we begin to find out what our identity really is. And I'd like to encourage you, that as we continue on this adventure, we will see how our identity makes sense in the fallen world that we are so immersed in. But let's go back to Hebrews 4:12 for a minute.

We read that one of the jobs of the word of God (the Bible) is that it "divides" soul from spirit. At first glance, it's kind of easy to read "divides soul and spirit" and not really wrestle with the meaning here. We might think: "Well, this is just a fancy way of saying the Bible is powerful and accomplishing great things." And that would be true, but it wouldn't be a very accurate understanding of what's being talked about here.

It's important that there is division between the soul and the spirit. As I mentioned before, they are supposed to serve very different functions, and when they get confused or are misused, then things can get very messy. And not only that, we can find it difficult to get clarity on our true identity.

The Greek word for soul here is *psuche*, which is pronounced "SOO-kay." This is the location where our minds, emotions, and will reside. And we need to take some time to really dig into just how profoundly our souls influence our lives.

Our Soulish Minds

Everything that is made is designed, and everything that is designed is meant to accomplish certain tasks. For example, I'm writing this book on my computer. It was designed to do this. It has keys with symbols on them, and when I push on one of them a certain kind of symbol pops up on the screen. If I put enough of those symbols together, I can create sentences that communicate something meaningful to others (at least I hope that's the case!) The design of my laptop is such that it's excellent in performing the task of writing.

But let's say I wanted to try something new. Given that I'm a reasonably adventurous person and I like to try things that are not what I'm used to doing, I decide to use my laptop to swat flies. I might get lucky and get rid of a few of those annoying critters, but I'm also going to be left with a computer that's no longer useful for writing letters or books because it's now laying on the floor in pieces. And on top of that disaster, I'm going to have to deal with all the dents that I've now put in my wall after using my computer for something it wasn't designed for.

I think you get my point (even if it's a little wacko).

Things that are designed, are designed for specific functions. And that's true of the soul. It's been designed by God with multiple tasks, and one of them is to *think*. The soul is where our minds work. This is quite a mystery really and one that has been wrestled with for centuries. We know that we have physical *brains*, but what about our *minds*? How do brains actually think?

The famous philosopher, Rene Descartes, suggested that the link between the physical brain and non-physical mind is through the pineal gland. This gland is found right in the middle of the brain, and today's medical advancements help us to understand that it's responsible for the regulation of the body's circadian rhythm which it accomplishes by secreting melatonin. But for someone like Descartes who was working with 17th century medicine, it was likely that he didn't really have a clear concept of the function of the pineal gland. To him, this gland was a mystery but since it was found right in the middle of the brain, it made sense to imagine that it was possibly the bridge between the physical brain and the non-physical mind.

It can sometimes be difficult to comprehend how something that has no physical attributes can affect another thing that is physical in nature. Maybe wind is a decent example here... you can't see wind but you can see its effects on objects. I live in a very windy part of the world, and in the spring, I can see evidence of the effects of wind in my backyard when I have to pick up all the broken twigs and branches that have been blown off my willow tree!

But I digress...

Our minds are what produces thoughts. They were designed by God to do so, and they do that extremely well. The thoughts they produce are incredibly diverse, touching on every aspect of human life. They are fearfully and wonderfully made! In fact, our minds have been on quite a run over the last number of centuries. Ever since the Enlightenment in the seventeenth–nineteenth centuries, the elevation of our human minds, including the exercising of reason and logic, has reached heights of celebrity never before seen in history. Our ability to think has become the central feature of what it means to be human. We have grown to depend on our minds as *the* means by which we navigate our way through life. We have become familiar, in our modern mindset, with tackling every problem first and foremost through the exercising of our minds. Most people don't even question this as it's become the norm.

We even try to use our minds to unravel things like our identities, and we end up finding barriers, and getting frustrated. This is primarily due to the fact that our minds are not actually functioning in the way they are supposed to. They're working hard, but they don't always work properly, as they were designed. The primary reason this is the case is because our minds (souls) were not meant to operate independently, in other words, on their own. They were meant to work in submission to God and His Spirit. Our soul-minds need to find their guidance from the Spirit of God and then process that direction into the nitty-gritty of life. One of the fruits of the Enlightenment is that people became so enamoured with human rationality that it seemed logical to eventually jettison God's involvement and guidance. As our souls became islands unto themselves, looking inwardly to self instead of outwardly to God, people became convinced that it was up to us to figure things out on our own. This still carries huge influence in people today, even within those who follow Jesus.

Proverbs 2:10 NASB says, "For wisdom will enter your heart, and knowledge will be pleasant to your soul..." Here we can see how knowing something, exercising thoughts to try and come to understandable conclusions, is associated with our souls. God designed our souls with the capacity to think. In a very real way our souls are like computer processors; the hardware exists to perform certain functions, but it requires data input before it can do anything. Without the information, there is nothing it can do. Which reminds me of a joke:

"One day a sorcerer challenged God. He said to God, 'I think I have the power to create things just like you. I challenge you to a creation contest!' Unfazed, God replied, 'OK, if you think you're that powerful, let's see what you can do. But remember, this is a challenge to create something out of nothing. Do you agree?' The sorcerer was so confident in his abilities that he immediately declared, 'Of course! I can use my powers to create anything out of nothing.' And so the sorcerer stepped outside, reached down and picked up a handful of dirt from which he was going to create something new and amazing, but God stopped him in his tracks and said, 'Hold on there, what are you doing?' The sorcerer looked surprised by the interruption and said wonderingly, 'What do you mean? I'm going to use this dirt to make something never seen before... something new from nothing!' God replied, 'OK that's all fine and good, but you need to get your own dirt!'"

That's how humans are made. We need to have some kind of input, a starting place, in order to do anything. The sorcerer thought he could make something out of nothing, but really he needed the dirt that already existed in order to create anything. The same is true for minds; they need input of some kind in order to create thoughts. We can't make thoughts out of nothing. Where our minds get the information becomes critical in discovering our identities because we can access good information and bad information. If our focus is on the world and the things that we can see and experience in the natural world, then our soul-minds will process conclusions based on that data. One of the things that we find when we do that, however, is that we struggle mightily to discover our identities... something is missing. But if we receive our information and direction from God (Spirit), then our soul-minds will process information primarily from Him, which will help us to understand the world in which we live much more clearly, and along with that we will also get clarity on who we really are. This is exactly what Paul was writing about in Romans 7:20. He was given a revelation from God about who he was in the midst of a broken and sinful world that even touched and affected a part of his own make-up.

So what does it mean to have soulish minds? I've already stated that our souls are where the mind functions, so it kind of makes sense to say that every mind is soulish. But what I'm meaning here is a little different.

When I say that a mind is soulish, I mean that it's thinking using the data that's being given to it, and in this case the mind is thinking about information from the world. A soulish mind is a worldly mind.

At a basic level, we need to understand that our minds process information from one of two places: it will process things that come from the *spirit* (God/supernatural), or it will process things from the *world* (information arising from the natural). The proper orientation of our soul-minds is that they would operate in submission to God's Spirit in order to receive pure information about what is good and true, and then use that information as the grid through which it applies that information to the natural world around it.

We live in such a secularized environment that to think about how this makes any sense is incredibly difficult. I mean, what do thoughts from God have to do with how I do my banking or how to plant seeds or how to drive my car? Living in the daily world requires me to think about things that are natural all the time, and it can seem that the supernatural has almost nothing to do with it. *But that is not actually the way we were designed, and it's not the way we find freedom.* Freedom comes when we submit to God's design. And He's inviting us to move, once again, into the kind of relationship with Him where we experience freedom to live as He made us to live. Thinking in submission to the Spirit of God does not mean that we won't still engage in the natural world around us. It just means that we will approach it from an entirely different starting point, with different perspectives and values. This is also true when we try to understand who we really are.

The real question here is this: *are we willing to simply accept that He wants us to think and live differently in order to live freely even if it doesn't make sense to us right now?* That's the challenge for us. We're being asked to submit our ways of thinking before Him in order for Him to begin rearranging our priorities and how we live. It's scary, and can even feel irresponsible, but by submitting to Him we will find a peace and freedom we couldn't have even imagined possible.

I've run the risk of only talking about our soul-minds here. The risk is that it may seem that I am agreeing with the elevation of human rationality to the detriment of our soul-emotion and our soul-will. It needs to be said that every part of our soul affects the other parts. Our thinking is affected by our emotions and our choices, and so on. But for the sake of brevity I only used the mind as our example. Our discussion includes the important principles of the distinction between our souls and spirits, and for now I'm trusting that this is enough for us to take some initial steps toward freedom in our identity. In the future, I hope to dive more deeply into the topics of our emotion and will, how they affect us, and how they too find their freedom in submission to the Spirit of God.

Understanding Our Nature: Being Spiritual and Being Natural

I've said many times, "words matter." Words carry meaning, and over time a word can begin to carry different meanings.

I've always been interested in how words and phrases come into being. For example, if you were to take great care in a delicate situation, you might be told to "handle it with kid gloves." Some of the finest leather used in making gloves come from the hide of a young goat called a "kid." This leather is extremely soft and thin, so if you do anything with these gloves, you must be very careful or they will tear.

The words we use are often coloured by the environment in which we use them. They are meant to convey meaning, but they also require great care in the use of them so they perform and communicate in a manner in which they were designed. The same is true when we talk about our souls and spirits.

Today, it's pretty common to hear someone describing the unseen world using the term "spiritual." I think it's an attempt to explain something that is not easily identified or clearly understood. But for some it still has value, and so the term "spiritual" is used to communicate something unseen but still holding value. This is a very broad term that usually points toward a religious belief, but it can be so wide-ranging in its meaning that it can include just about anything that doesn't really fit into our science-based modern world. Because this sense of being spiritual is so ambiguous, it's easy to imagine that anything that has some kind of existence, but is not easily seen or quantified by our senses, can be determined as spiritual. This vague understanding allows people to think that when the Bible talks about soul and spirit, they are basically the same thing. They are both spiritual. But that would be very far from the truth.

First Corinthians 2 is an excellent place to go when we want to get a little more understanding about our souls and our spirits. Paul was writing to the Corinthians, who were just learning about what it meant to be disciples of Jesus. It would be an understatement to say they were having some trouble in understanding who they were in Christ. Their church was a mess! I've pastored a few churches over the years, and I've seen some pretty challenging situations, but this Corinthian church was on another level.

In the early chapters of the first book written to the Corinthians, Paul was expressing some pretty blunt evaluations of the state of this people's faith. One of the issues being addressed was division between people in the church over who was worthy of being followed. Some said they were followers of Paul, and some were followers of another apostle named Apollos. In the end, Paul says they are entirely off base in engaging in these types of arguments.

Paul was trying to break through their confusion by telling them there was a better way to live, and specifically, a better way to gain understanding. He told them that when he came to them, he didn't hide his weaknesses, but instead relied entirely on the Holy Spirit to prove the power of God which could convince people that the message was directly from Him. In this, he mentioned wisdom many times, and differentiated between human wisdom and God's wisdom.

One would think that wisdom is wisdom wherever it is to be found, but that wouldn't be true. There is an earthly kind of wisdom and a heavenly kind of wisdom, and the means to discern these two different things requires different kinds of tools. For example, a soul is designed by God to receive data and then to process it to reach conclusions. A soul doesn't have the innate capacity to determine on its own whether the data it's processing is good or bad; it simply processes what it receives. This might seem counterintuitive given that we think about good things and bad things all the time. But my point here is this: a soul that has been immersed in sin right from its inception and has had no experience of anything outside of this reality, will not, on its own, be able to discern that the information it's processing from the world it finds itself in, is actually bad/sinful or good/holy. Something outside of itself is needed to show that there is more than what it currently processes whether it's thoughts, emotions, or will.

Because we have lived within our souls our entire lives, the manner in which we engage our world around us is how it has always been for each of us. Before we had any self-awareness, our minds were processing our environments. We were learning about our parents' faces; we were learning about how our bodies work. And when we get a little older, we start to process our emotions; we start to deal with feelings for others that bring a sense of exhilaration and frustration all at the same time. Processing, processing.

Then we learn about how our choices work. We begin to see that some things are understood by others as being good and some things are bad. And then, one day, we find ourselves wanting to choose something we have been taught is bad… how do we handle this? Through experience. We sometimes choose badly and then have to live through consequences. We begin to see how others, and even ourselves, are like those ancient Greek actors called "hypocrites," and we learn about deception and the pain that can come our way.

This is all being processed by our souls, all the time. The amount of data is astounding.

A fish doesn't know what it means to be dry because it has been wet its entire existence. In the same way, a soul, on its own, doesn't know how to process in such a way that it can discern godly wisdom, because it has always been immersed in sin. David said in Psalm 51:5 NIV: "Surely I was sinful at birth, sinful from the time my mother conceived me." David's soul only knew how to operate with the data that was tainted by sin because that is the only kind of data it ever processed. The same is true for each and every soul that has ever lived after the original Adam.

I share this with you because it's an important aspect of knowing who you are and knowing how your soul and spirit function. What I have described above is the reality for anyone who has never accepted Jesus as Saviour. For those, their souls are living in a sin-infused reality that makes them unable to understand, accept, or process the wisdom that comes from God. To them, it sounds like foolishness. One other thing that I will show you in future chapters, is that *your* soul is still wrestling with the effects of sin, and this has massive implications on how you think and feel about your identity in Jesus. I want you to know this because I'm convinced that when you hear about these dynamics, you will be encouraged and will see that a freedom for you exists that you may not have ever thought possible. Stay tuned.

Being a Natural Person

Paul says in 1 Corinthians 2:14 NASB that "...a natural man does not accept the things of the Spirit of God; for they are foolishness to him, and he cannot understand them, because they are spiritually appraised."

Paul uses the term "natural man" here. The Greek word is *psuchikos* (SOO-kick-ohs), which means "natural soul or mind." This natural soul is designed to engage in information from the natural world, the physical world around us. And there is nothing wrong with that insofar as it is performing what it is meant to do by utilizing the tools of mind, emotion, and will in the world it finds itself in.

But the world it finds itself in is *broken,* and it has been broken right from the beginning of its existence, and this has a dramatic effect on how it operates.

A natural man, or *psuchikos,* is someone who cannot accept or understand the things of God. Why? Because the soul will process whatever information it's given. If it's given natural or carnal information that has been tainted by sin, it will come to conclusions based on that fallen and worldly data. A natural soul, or one that has been immersed in a sin-filled existence from birth, will not properly process spiritually based information that comes from God. That's why Paul says that a *psuchikos,* or a naturally led man, will not be able to accept the things of God. In fact, they will simply seem foolish to him.

But the person who is not *psuchikos* or soul-led, is one who is instead *pneumaticos* (new-MAT-i-cos) or spirit-led. This is what Paul calls the person in 1 Corinthians 2:15 NASB: "...he who is spiritual...", and this changes the whole playing field. Why is that the case? Because if we are soul-led, all we can do is grapple with our own best thoughts. We can only access information that is available to us, and for a soul-led person that means that we are only open to what people can come up with on their own or *naturally*. And this can be pretty good a lot of the time. Consider our modern medical system and health care in general; it has come a long way, and if we are sick, then it can seem to be a pretty good option... until it isn't. For many people, disease and sickness is a chronic reminder of the limitations of human ingenuity. When God made the soul, He created something that is simply astounding with an amazing capacity to accomplish things. But the soul was never meant to be our source of life.

Even as I write this, I feel compelled to clarify something... we can live our lives as saved people and still be very *soulish*, that is, relying primarily on our souls to lead us through life depending on our reason and logic to figure things out as we go. But the soul was never meant to *lead* us! That's our spirit's job, and when we reject our spirit as our primary guide, we find ourselves feeling like we live very distant from God. And this is much more than just a feeling because the *life of God* within us is meant to provide very real power and insight to help us live a full and abundant life. Most Christians I know think that when we talk about living with the source of life within us, we think about Jesus having saved us (forgiven our sins), so we can one day be with Him after we die. Not a false thought, but it is a severely truncated idea. The source of life, that is the *zoe* life of God, is that which creates life out of nothing! It is the expression of God's power to change and transform. We are not to live led by our fallen souls; instead we are to be led by our invigorated and powerful spirits that have been made new and have direct access to God Himself. We have God's *zoe* life within us, and it's meant to have impact in every aspect of our daily lives. This is meant to be the reality of our lives as saved people in Christ.

Our souls have been made with incredible capacity, but that capacity has been catastrophically affected by sin. To be clear, they were never meant to be the means through which our lives find meaning and purpose; through which we access the needed information and wisdom to live, no. Instead, our souls are meant to be the bridge, so to speak, between the supernatural (God our creator/sustainer/provider) and natural (the world we live in).

The soul is to be the *receiver* of the information from God and then its function is to live in constant obedience to the spirit (our spirit that is one with God's Spirit). In this state of service to the spirit, our souls then process the many different ways that we should live. The third part of what constitutes a human being, that being our physical bodies, is to live in obedience to our souls (mind, emotion, and will). Our bodies then become instruments through which our souls express their desires.

So what I'm presenting here is the idea that we were originally designed to be spirit-led people, connected to God's life alive in us, and having our souls guided by this source of life. Spirit is the master; soul is the bridge; and body is the expression. But is this just something I came up with on my own, or does it have merit beyond my own thoughts? I think the heart and intent of God will lead us to a place where we can see His invitation into a spirit-led life is real, and that it has been the case right from the beginning.

CHAPTER 3:

What Is the Spirit?

IN THIS CHAPTER WE are going to be talking about spirit which includes the spirit of a person and also the Holy Spirit of God. In the last chapter, I mentioned that people are to be *pneumaticos* or spirit-led people. Of course this implies that there is a part of us that is spirit, or at least, that a part of us has a space where spirit may reside in real and practical ways. Both are actually true. We *have* a spirit, and a *Spirit* resides within us. We need to consider both of these truths in more detail.

At the very beginning of recorded history, we see that the Holy Spirit of God was real and active in the world. In Genesis 1:2 NASB we read that the Holy Spirit was "...moving over the surface of the waters." This indicates that the Holy Spirit is real and has the capacity to do things.

We can see quite an array of activity that the Holy Spirit does in Scripture.

We see Him convicting people of sin (John 16:8–11); regenerating people (Peter 1:4); baptizing individuals (1 Cor. 12:13);

indwelling (Romans 8:9); and in various other passages He fills, empowers, assures, illuminates, teaches, and gives gifts. For our purposes I want to focus on how He regenerates and indwells people.

Holy Spirit and Us

When we think of things that can cause devastation, we conjure up images of hurricanes wreaking havoc on coastal cities like New Orleans, in 2005, when hurricane Katrina caused upwards of 70 billion dollars in damage. Or we think of the mega earthquake of 2011, that occurred off the eastern coast of Japan. This monster was recorded to be a magnitude of 9.1, lasted six minutes, and produced a massive tsunami that caused the death of 20,000 people, and produced damage to the tune of 360 billion dollars (USD)!

Our capacity to comprehend the extent of devastating human loss is stretched to its limit when we allow ourselves to think about the millions upon millions of lives lost in the numerous wars that have been fought in the 20th century alone.

But as horrendous as these events are, they literally pale in comparison to the absolute demolition of humanity experienced through the onslaught of sin. Everything that God created as an expression of life has been tainted with shadowy darkness. Sin is the antithesis of life. It's the parasitic presence that has no capacity to exist except for its ability to sink its tentacles into the essence of life itself and twist what was made beautiful. Once sin has accomplished its task, it has no ability, or essence within itself, to continue existing... the life that it latches onto is, in fact, the scaffold upon which sin has its ability to operate. Once it produces death, it destroys the scaffold, and enacts its own demise. Sin is so death inducing that it ultimately produces its own self-destruction. The only way that sin and death continues is because the life of God continues to this very day.

So imagine the life that was breathed into Adam. This is the life-breath of God Himself that was His power to infuse into Adam the very essence of being that caused him to become animated and to function as the image-bearing creature He was meant to be. Adam was, in a very real way, the image of God walking the face of the earth.

He was endowed with great wisdom and creativity. At the very beginning of all created things, God gave Adam this wonderful task: Every animal that God had created was to come before Adam to be named. We read this in Genesis 2:19 NASB, "And out of the ground the Lord God formed every beast of the field and every bird of the sky, and brought them to the man to see what he would call them; and whatever the man called a living creature, that was its name."

What an amazing event! God created a human being to share in His own character traits, having creative thought, emotions, and desires, and then, as part of this wonderful relationship, God gave Adam this great honour of naming all the creatures that He had just formed from the dust. We are not told that God put any parameters or boundaries on Adam, He just said to name them, and once they were named, it was a done deal. It may seem a small thing, but if you imagine the unbelievable reality of what is going on, you begin to see just how elevated Adam was in God's eyes.

God had just formed out of dirt, every animal and bird. The sheer magnitude of this event is astounding. Adam is surrounded by this cacophony of noises: Elephants are blaring; cheetahs are running like the wind blowing through the grass; birds are flying everywhere, chirping and singing; pigs are snorting, and wolves are howling. You get the picture. Each one was made by God with the same care He made everything else. It was perfection. And then He said to Adam, "Now I want you to name each one. I want you to put your stamp upon what I have created. I want to *share* this with you. Since I have created all things and I have made you to be like Me, I want you to share in this new beginning by being a co-creator of sorts... you name each creature, and I will accept whatever name you choose." Incredible.

This is an example of just how good Adam was created; every part of him was in alignment with God. There was no sin; nothing was out of place. Adam was made a perfect human being bearing similarities to God Himself. These elements are so important for us to understand because what God made in Adam is what He is aiming to restore at the end of human history when Jesus returns to make all things new again. What was made in perfection in the garden, and was lost through sin, will be reclaimed in the end.

What's incredible to imagine is that though we currently wrestle with sin, *we* are being invited into a similar relationship with God that Adam enjoyed! We're being asked to be co-creators bearing God's image and speaking into reality the things of God's heart. We're being invited into really knowing ourselves and engaging in living in the identity we've been given through Jesus and the Holy Spirit who lives within us. We've been given this task of pulling back the veil of our hidden identities and to come out of our struggles in order to live in light and be people who shine this light of Jesus to others around us.

In order to accomplish this, we need to know how we are built and what's really going on that creates our realities. We know that we struggle but why? We know that Adam was created perfect, and that we aren't, but how does that really work? What does it mean to be a co-creator with God? If we're honest with ourselves, it probably seems more than enough of a task just to make it through our day sometimes, let alone creating something of the kingdom of God around us or even more, within ourselves!

One of my goals is to help you to see bigger than just survival mode. I believe that God Himself is calling you to see yourself in the light of Adam, to see just how blessed you are, and what that actually means for knowing who you really are. God wants you to live in Him and in *freedom*! So let's continue by looking at how Adam was built and what that meant for him.

The Life in Adam

In Genesis 2:7 it says that God made the first human being out of dust. He formed the man, gave him shape and structure. God knit together all of Adam's tissues and sinews. Adam was given his form and *became*. But he was not yet complete because God wanted Adam to be made in His own image, and that required something that a physical form alone was not able to accomplish.

After God made Adam's physical form, He then did something immensely important. *He breathed into Adam.* But this was not any kind of breath like you see when someone is breathing in cold weather with steamy clouds coming out of their mouths. What God breathed here was infused with power, it was *the breath of life*!

If you look at Genesis 2:7 in more detail, you see God breathing the breath of life (spirit) into Adam, and he became a living soul (nephesh). The Hebrew word used for "breath of life" here is *nismat*, which is used in Genesis 7:22 to talk of the "breath of the spirit" and in Proverbs 20:27 as the "spirit of man," which it goes on to say is "the lamp of the Lord."

The spirit of man is the lamp of the Lord.

A lamp is something used to illuminate. It's meant to shine light in order to brighten surroundings so things can be seen. What was once not seen is now seen. And a lamp must have a source of power in order to be able to do the job it was designed for. So when we read that the Lord breathed into Adam his *spirit*, it looks as though this was meant to be a part of him that allowed the presence of the Lord to reside in such a manner that He would be able to shine light into Adam in order to show him things that he couldn't see without this light.

It says in John 4:24 NASB that "God is spirit; and those who worship him must worship in spirit and truth." This has always been an interesting passage to me. In the past when I heard "God is spirit," in practical terms, it really just meant that God was different than me. He is higher, purer, perfect; really it just meant that God is way above and beyond me. And then the passage in John talks about how I am supposed to worship Him, but I'm supposed to worship Him "in spirit," and this somehow means that I will be doing that truthfully. To be honest, this seemed like one of those Christian phrases that sounded elevated and better than what I'm familiar with, but I didn't really understand how to actually grasp the meaning or how it was supposed to affect me.

Truth has always been something that I have engaged with my mind. In that sense it has been a *soulish* task. My mind is something found in my soul, and I use it to process information about my world. It's where I discover things and figure things out. *So why couldn't I understand this thing about worshipping God in spirit and truth?* It seemed like just another problem that my mind was supposed to figure out and then I would know the *truth* about it. But a big part of the problem was that I was using my mind (a part of my soul) to discover the truth about spirit-related things. This meant that I was trying to use my soul-mind to discover things it was not designed for. Why do I say this?

Isaiah 55:8 NASB says, "For My thoughts are not your thoughts" And then in verse 9 God continues by saying that His thoughts are much "higher" than our thoughts. If I combine this with the fact that God is spirit by his nature, then what we have here is that the reason that God's thoughts are higher than ours is because they partake of *His nature*; they are *Spirit-thoughts*. They are of a different composition and purpose than what my limited soul-mind can comprehend. It's not that God's thoughts are only more complex and elevated than what my soul-mind can process; *they are of a whole different nature.*

Now let's remember that God is inviting us into a worshipping relationship with Him. He has in mind that this relationship is beautiful and deep and fulfilling. In every sense it's meant to be *true*. This is more than just a distinction between something that's correct or false, like an answer on an exam. The truth we are invited into here has elements of all things that are right and good. It is a comprehensive *rightness* that allows things like joy and peace and strength to reside. We need to remember that God is inviting us, with the expectation to enjoy this with Him. But we can't access it if we try and use our soulishly limited minds to get there. We need something different. So what is that thing?

It is our spirit.

This is what God has given to us, just like He gave to Adam. Our spirit is the place where the "lamp of God" illuminates us. It's the place where we commune with Him and His light is allowed to shine its brilliance over our whole life, including our souls and along with that our minds. Our soul-mind was never meant to be elevated above our spirit because that would mean that it has taken on the pride-filled task of evaluating the things and thoughts of God. But God Himself has already told us that *His* thoughts are way above ours! The only way we can worship Him *truthfully* is to do so in spirit.

But how? That is a great question and one that I want to explore. Suffice it to say that we begin in a way that our minds don't usually operate or *want* to operate. We begin with a little thing called *humility*. Second Chronicles 7:14 says that if we humble ourselves and pray, seek the face of God, and turn from our wicked ways, He will hear our prayer and pour out healing on us through forgiveness and healing on our lands and the things that cause hurt and pain.

Truly understanding ourselves requires spirit knowledge that can only come to us if we humbly submit ourselves to the Spirit of God. True knowledge comes first through saying, "I don't know." Pretty counterintuitive, isn't it?

I think our current discussion about our soul-mind and spirit understanding is helped along through this passage in 2 Chronicles 7:14. If we choose to *humble ourselves*, in the context of our discussion, that means that we recognize that our use of our soul-minds to try and figure out our relationship with God, as our first and only way of discovering truth, will, in the end, be an exercise of pride. We must humble ourselves and admit that our own thinking and trying to figure things out is not where we begin. We say to God, "I *don't* know and I want to know, so please forgive me and help me."

I think then God says to us, "If you really want to know, then start by *seeking My face*. Pursue being with Me, and I will begin to reveal what I want you to know." Now we see that *relationship* and *humility* are actually essential in understanding what is true. These are not categories that our minds use in order to logically and rationally discover things. God's ways and thoughts are different...

We need to repent of our soul-mind pride and talk to God about all this (pray). We need to actively seek His *face*. It's in seeking His face that we will actually begin to see the things we long for. And this includes the knowledge that we seek. Seeking God's face means that we want to see Him; listen to Him; be taught by Him; share with Him, and receive from Him. It's putting ourselves into *His* agenda and off of our own. It's to submit to His way of thinking, and sacrificing our own well-used pathways of soulish knowledge. And when we do this, we put ourselves in a position where it's now our *spirit* that begins to communicate the things of God because God Himself is speaking there! This is what Adam experienced, and it's simply wonderful.

It would seem from this passage that God created Adam with a physical body and then breathed both a spirit and a soul into him. Adam became infused with *ruach* or spirit, and this was accompanied with a *nephesh* or a soul. For the purposes of this book, I am not taking on the nuanced discussion about how both *ruach* and *nephesh* can sometimes be used interchangeably in the Old Testament, which gives rise to the question of whether Adam had a spirit and a separate soul when God breathed into him, or whether Adam simply had a spirit/soul (immaterial aspect) and body (physical aspect). My take on this is that given some of the ambiguity found in the Old Testament, we can look to the New Testament for clarity and read that back into the Old. I think this is reasonable given that there is no indication in Scripture that God somehow altered the make-up of humanity from the Old to the New Testaments. When we look at the big picture and take in what we find in the Bible as a whole, there is a strong case to be made that when God created Adam, He made him with a spirit and a separate soul and a physical body.

The fact that the Hebrew categories of soul/spirit don't always fit neatly into our New Testament understandings does not change how Adam lives in alignment with God, and here is the most important thing to remember: Adam was living without sin, and so his soul (mind, emotion, and will) was performing in perfect harmony with God (who is Spirit).

We know that Adam could hear and know God's intentions because he told Adam to live with the intent to be fruitful and to multiply (Gen. 1:28); God told Adam what things he had been given as food to eat (Gen. 1:29). And He told Adam the consequences of eating from the forbidden tree (Gen. 2:16–17). We see very clear evidence of how close Adam (and then Eve) lived with God in 3:8–13, where a very clear dialogue is taking place in the garden between God (who was walking there, being present) and Adam and Eve.

It seems pretty clear that the original design of God was that human beings were given life and that life was to be lived out under the guidance and direction of God who is Spirit. So what can we take away from this?

I'd like you to hold in your minds the following brief description of what living in the fullness of your identity in God looks like:

Spirit is to be over all things. Spirit is the master guide. God is Spirit and therefore He is the ultimate provider, sustainer, teacher and guide for life. All created things are to fall under the authority of Spirit. This means much more than just a belief statement. This is to be a whole-life submission to the Spirit of God in all things.

Adam is created with a soul that is designed to live under the authority of Spirit and was also given a physical body which was meant to function under the authority of his soul. The body is meant to obey what the soul commands. Thinking (logic and reasoning capacity of the soul), along with emotion (feelings, desires, and appetites), and will (ability to make choices), are meant to guide the actions of the body. Given that Adam's soul was sinless, his soul was guided by the present authority of God's Spirit, and then his body was able to perform all the things that bring delight to God as Adam's sinless soul gave direction.

And on top of all of that, *Adam was able to live in absolute and total freedom in his identity as an image bearer of God, with his body in obedient service to his soul, and his soul in obedient service to the Spirit.*

But all that changed...

Voices Matter

I remember being at gatherings or events where there were a lot of people and being able to hear my dad's voice over all the hubbub. Well, not necessarily *over* everything else. It wasn't as though my dad had a voice that was many decibels louder than everyone else's; it's just that my ears were tuned to hear him. Especially his laugh. I remember when he would laugh, it wouldn't matter if I was on the other side of the room, and people were shouting or talking or laughing, I could hear his voice crystal clear.

I didn't realize it at the time, but that voice brought me a lot of comfort. I knew that it was connected to the one who watched over me, took care of me, provided for me, played catch with me, and guided me in life. It didn't matter that a lot of other voices were in the room because I heard my dad's voice over them all.

You have probably heard it said how important it is that we hear God's voice over all the other voices that vie for our attention in the world around us. We know that if we listen to the voices that are not in alignment with God, we put ourselves in very dangerous positions. *What voice we listen to matters an awful lot!*

This is certainly true for Adam.

God had told Adam not to eat from one tree in the garden. *Only one!* He had total access to every single tree and plant but just not that one. This tree was called the tree of the knowledge of good and evil, and if he ate from it, something unthinkable would happen... Adam would die. He would fall from his place of existing as the perfect human being. He would suffer loss that he couldn't yet imagine. His entire life would change and not for the better. He would live in struggle for the rest of his time on earth.

I have wondered if this tree's fruit had within it the power to bring Adam into a place of realization that he previously didn't know, or if it simply was the eating of the fruit that would confirm a decision that Adam had made, that was not in alignment with God. If Adam chose to eat it, then the eaten fruit was just the evidence that Adam had gone astray. He had given into evil, and so now he knew both good (what he had before) and evil (the reality of agreeing with a sinful influence). Either way the result is the same... death. And this death occurred because *Adam had chosen to listen to a voice other than God's.*

Satan had already influenced Eve with a lie. He told her that if she ate from the forbidden tree she would then be like God. But she was *already like God*! She had been made in his image! But because she listened to a voice other than God's, it influenced her decisions, and it influenced her *soul*. Indirectly, Satan's voice influenced Adam's soul as well, and the result was sin and ultimately death.

Here is what has taken place in a nutshell:

- God, who is Spirit, creates Adam, the first human who was made to be the apex of creation and be in a special relationship with God.
- God as Spirit breathes a spirit and soul into Adam, which allows Adam the capacity to live with a similar nature to God Himself. This is the Adam made in God's *likeness*.
- God's Spirit, communing with Adam's spirit, was to be the master provider over Adam and his soul.
- Adam's soul was then to be the master over his body which would obey the commands given by his soul.
- Then Sin occurred:
- Adam's soul listens to and obeys a voice other than God's.
- Adam's relationship with God is now distanced, and he becomes much more reliant on his own soul for direction as opposed to God's Spirit.
- Adam can still hear God's voice, but the reality is that sin now exists in Adam, and this causes the battle within him as to what voice to listen to: his own, others' or God's. Where Adam once lived in perfect union with God in the garden, he now must struggle to hear and obey God. And the distance from God that Adam now feels is something that will increase over the generations.

We see this progression of the disease of sin that corrupts people's souls continuing throughout time until we get to Genesis 6:11–12 AMP that highlights just how bad things had gotten. "The earth was depraved and putrid in God's sight, and the land was filled with violence (desecration, infringement, outrage, assault, and lust for power). And God looked upon the world and saw how degenerate, debased, and vicious it was, for all humanity had corrupted their way upon the earth and lost their true direction."

It's not a stretch to imagine that what is described in Genesis 6:11–12 was *not* the original intent of God when He created Adam. What He desired was that Adam's soul would stay obedient to the Spirit's voice and in that place of service Adam would continue to live in absolute *freedom to be who he was created to be*, enjoying God's presence and experiencing all the manifest goodness of God and His blessings.

But when Adam chose to listen to a voice that was in opposition to God, *it elevated his own soul above God's Spirit*; it was an act that was born out of twisted logic, tainted emotions, and confused will... this was Adam's very *self*-acting in rebellion against God. It not only brought about the dramatic shortening of Adam's life, but it affected generations that followed to the point where all people were corrupted and living in violent depravity.

Listening to God's voice, and living in the rightly ordered life with our souls under the authority of God's Spirit, is where we find life and our truest identity. It's where we find freedom and peace. Listening to the voice of God is so important that God Himself didn't give up speaking loudly to humanity... His cry of invitation back to Him came through many different judges, prophets, priests, kings, and leaders who were obedient to God. None of them were perfect as Adam once was way back in the days of that pristine garden, but the call that began the journey back into relationship with God remained.

And it remains to this day.

We must now venture into the New Testament to begin to dig into what God is saying to us about our own journeys. We need to begin to understand our struggle for freedom and identity through what He says in His Word, and we are invited to see what our lives can look like when our souls, once again, live in obedience to the Spirit of God.

CHAPTER 4:
The Struggle

"What is causing the quarrels and fights among you? Don't they come from the evil desires at war within you? You want what you don't have, so you scheme and kill to get it. You are jealous of what others have, but you can't get it, so you fight and wage war to take it away from them. Yet you don't have what you want because you don't ask God for it. And even when you ask, you don't get it because your motives are all wrong–you want only what will give you pleasure. You adulterer! Don't you realize that friendship with the world makes you an enemy of God? I say it again: if you want to be a friend of the world, you make yourself an enemy of God. Do you think the Scriptures have no meaning? They say that God is passionate that the spirit he has placed within us should be faithful to him. And he gives grace generously. As the Scriptures say, 'God opposes the proud but gives grace to the humble.' So humble yourselves before God. Resist the devil, and he will flee from you. Come close to God, and God will come close to you. Wash your hands, you sinners; purify your hearts, for your loyalty is divided between God and the world. Let there be tears for what you have done. Let there be sorrow and deep grief. Let there be sadness instead of laughter,

and gloom instead of joy. Humble yourselves before the Lord, and he will lift you up in honor" (James 4:1–10 NLT).

ISN'T IT KIND OF crazy how we can know something is good for us but still pursue the opposite thing because we want it more? I know that it's not very good for my mind or my body if I spend too much time sitting in front of the TV and vegging on my couch. But when I come home from a long day, have supper, and begin to think about my evening, it seems like my whole mind and body *yearn* to sit in my recliner and snack and snooze! I wouldn't be exaggerating when I say that a veritable stream of justifications flow through me, including thoughts and emotions, to suggest that this is the *only* option for me. I won't try to describe them because they are different for everyone, but suffice it to say that it is real.

This is Romans 7:20 all over again. I do the things I don't want to do. But here is the kicker... it seems that I'm actually doing the thing I *do* want to do, but that's the thing that's bad for me. The good thing I should do, whether it's exercise, yardwork, reading, praying, or some other productive and beneficial activity, just feels like the last thing I want to do. Why is that?

Because there is a war going inside of us.

God tells us exactly this in James 4:1–10. Here it describes believers who are struggling with all kinds of battles. They are arguing with each other; they are upset and fighting, and generally there is no peace at all. James doesn't get into the details about what the issues were, but it doesn't take too much of an imagination to think of how conflicts and arguments exist in the church. I know I have been on the receiving end of a good number of these darts, and to my chagrin, I have launched toward others more than I like to admit.

Do you want to know something? The reason these battles exist is because followers of Jesus, too often, don't know who they really are. They're confused about their identity in Jesus. They don't have an understanding of the new creation they are. *They are still at war.*

I have mentioned a few times that the purpose of this book is to help us to know who we really are in Jesus so we can have peace (no more war) and freedom (unrestrained to really live). One of the things we need to begin to accept is that there are underlying forces that motivate us in our lives that really affect our ability to freely embrace and live out our identities found in Jesus.

Motive Matters

James points out that the believers he's addressing are experiencing all kinds of conflicts in their relationships with each other, along with battles being waged internally
because their motives are all messed up.

They were caught up in the trap of trying to fight for their places, whether it was opinions about what was right and wrong or more basic attempts to try and simply elevate themselves in the eyes of their peers. I'm sure there were many conversations taking place that were much more inclined to tear down others rather than build them up. When things get reduced to a dog-eat-dog existence, you learn pretty quickly that you had better grow big teeth, and those teeth are kinds of arguments and tactics used to tear people apart.

All of this arises from motives from within. All of our actions are prompted by an internal dialogue taking place in our souls. For example, if I try to tear someone down through criticism or lies, then I have already agreed with a game plan that was orchestrated by my mind, emotion, and will. If I feel threatened by someone, then I will try and neutralize the threat. I may think about ways to undermine their character or lie about them in a way that makes others believe what I want them to believe. Or, I may be much more subtle, and simply try to paint a picture of how I was somehow wronged. If I can bring that person onto my side, then I have experienced a win that my wounded soul takes as a justification for my actions.

And again, it's not only my mind working alone here. In fact, before my mind has time to really think things through, my emotions rise up to add passion and urgency to the mix. Sprinkle in a little jealousy and pride, and all of a sudden my mind is coming up with ideas to grow my dog teeth just a little bigger and sharper so I can tear my opponent to pieces, either aggressively or subtly. But my mind and emotion together still lack what is needed to accomplish the task at hand, because I still need to put into action my diabolic plan. Enter my will. Once my mind has justified a course of action, and my emotion has cemented it with a passionate energy, then my will is needed to put everything into motion, and so I make the choice to gossip or lie about my enemy in order to protect myself from the threat. Please remember here that I am talking about followers of Jesus as that is exactly who the apostle James is talking to in James chapter 4.

It's pretty hard to live in a community when the goal is to tear apart everyone around you. It doesn't matter if you do this from a place of deep woundedness in your soul; it doesn't matter if you protect yourself by loudly opposing others or through speaking with a gentle voice that seduces others into agreeing with you in your woundedness. In all this the *style* that is used ends up in the same result: destruction for others and destruction within my own soul. And the beat goes on...

The crazy thing is this: When we are caught up in the frenzy of this way of life, it can seem almost impossible to imagine any other option. Sometimes we become aware of just how nuts it is to live this way when we see the pain that we have caused or endured, and that maybe there is a brighter path. But something rises up within us to oppose this tiny glimmer of light. Just when we think there must be a better way, or maybe it's the idea that we *hope* there is a better way, this sense, not even a thought really but an underlying sense that guides a course of action, says to us that it's impossible to overcome what seems to be the way of the world. And so our wounded souls cry out that our *only* choice is to fight harder, in the attempt to try to protect ourselves.

Protect? This is the last thing we are actually doing. In fact, we are exposing ourselves to an enemy who is revelling in the destruction that our souls are causing, and in the end we reap what we sow... more pain, more disillusionment, more hatred, more wounds, more death, and much less freedom.

Now, remember the apostle James is talking to a group of followers of Jesus, and I'm speaking in the same vein. When I say that we experience the sting of death, I don't mean that we are not saved but that we are experiencing a lie, and that lie is the means through which the devil tries to convince us that our identities are truly tied to our soulish experiences, to worldly ways, to hurts, pains, and loss. In this, he convinces us that we really aren't the children of God because if we were we would *never* do these things! If we agree with him, then we cause our experience of our truest identity in Jesus to be hidden from us, and our souls feel entirely lost. The truth of the matter is that we haven't lost our identity because that remains in our spirit. But we lose the *experience* of our identity. We aren't living as God made us, and it seems like He's a million miles away from us. He really has made us new creations in Christ, and we have been made alive, but what we are doing and experiencing is anything but life sometimes.

The reason is because we are living with our focus on our souls, being *soul led* and not *spirit led*, where our new identity in Jesus resides. If we are soul led, then we put our focus on the things of this world... in this case, what other people are saying about us, or the promotion we didn't receive because of a boss who has it in for us, or the actions of someone who betrayed us on some deep level. Remember, our souls can only process what they receive, and so if we choose to receive all the garbage of this broken world, then it will process garbage responses, and in this we experience death not life.

There is a longing built into our souls that desire better, and that's why there's so much confusion and pain when we don't live under the authority of the spirit, and that's why it's so important to have our eyes fixed on the things of God instead of the things of this world. We long for better, for peace, for freedom, but can't find it in ourselves. We struggle and fight to try and carve out a better life, but if we live soul led, we end up just recycling the broken things around us and in us. Our motives then become selfish, and we create dynamics of competition instead of community.

Living as Adulterers

I think we have a hard time understanding just how much God loves us. He created humanity out of a pure desire to have totally free fellowship with us. It must have hurt Him deeply when Adam and Eve fell out of fellowship because in His mind it was just so beautiful.

This love is so deep and so profound that it motivates everything God does. If He describes Himself as "love" (1 John 4:16), then it stands to reason that He would have created everything out of a motivation of love. God's love has built within it selflessness and blessing. It exists and acts out of a desire to see good done for others. It is loyal to its principles all the way down and provides a safe place of intimacy where nothing needs to be hidden.

I think that's why God uses such strong language to describe His followers who are not living in love, *adulterers* (James 4:4). To commit adultery is to betray someone who has shared close intimacy with you. Everything has been laid bare, and all has been entrusted. Trust has been displayed based on selflessness and care. This is how God desires for a relationship with us. So when people act sel*fish*ly instead of sel*fless*ly, it's an act of betrayal to God. Instead of exhibiting selfless love, it becomes selfish love or love of myself. We have elevated ourselves and what we can get for ourselves over God and what He desires to share with us. We *take*. God *gives*.

Whenever we live as soul-led people, even as followers of Jesus, we try and take. We become just like the people described in James 4:1–10. Our motives get all out of whack, and we think this is just the way the world is as though it's an inevitable reality. But the truth is, it's not inevitable; it's just that a lie has taken up our view. We can change the world by believing that *we* can change. But so often we choose to live as friends of this world instead of as friends of God. War happens when two nations want to protect or gain what they see as most valuable but can't get it unless the other backs down. Since neither will back down, the only option is to duke it out.

War, whether it's between two nations, or between two people, or between an individual's soul and spirit, is simply *not inevitable*. There is an alternative, and Jesus is that alternative. Because He has saved us and has given us new life and new identity in Him, we have the capacity to live in freedom from war, around us and within us. *But it matters where we choose to live.* If we live in our exalted souls as our master, we will have to fight, and we will fight out of selfish motives. And let me be clear here: this is the reality of many saved Christians who haven't yet learned how to live as spirit-led instead of soul-led people. But if we live with our spirit as our guide, we will find increasing peace. And we will see that our identity in Jesus is truly the way.

We can see evidence of this when James describes the options available to the believers he is writing to. He says they can be friends of the world, but if they do, they will be living as enemies of God. They will not be living in their true identity but instead will be living a lie, a false self. They still belong to God, but their *experience* will be as enemies of God. God is filled with jealousy for our spirits that He placed within us (James 4:5). He's jealous because He wants this aspect of us to rise up and guide us. He knows that the spirit within a believer has been made alive by the presence of His Holy Spirit, and this part of us will draw us back to Himself. It's by our spirit, and Holy Spirit's presence there, that we see the alternative we were talking about before. It's through our spirit that we see that letting down our guards, stopping our selfish attacks, ending our cloying attempts to woo others to our side, and ceasing to be a warring people is not weakness or foolishness but is instead exactly what heaven desires. It's the wisdom of God motivated by the love of God. Even if it means losing the battle before us. Even if it means that my character gets smeared. Even if it means that I don't get the promotion. Even if it means that I lose my argument. Even if it makes me look foolish... I am only looking foolish to worldly ways of thinking and acting. I think Jesus did exactly this in life and on the cross. Foolishness to the world but a powerful expression of the love of God in action to heaven.

Lord help us to live in our true identities! Help us to live in freedom from the world. Help us to live with our eyes on Jesus so that our spirits may be our guide and our souls can function as You designed them.

God's Action Plan For Us

If you're like me, you may be wondering about how to actually live led by your spirit/Holy Spirit instead of by your soul. There is a way that is pointed out to us in verse 6 of James 4, and it says this: "...God is opposed to the proud, but gives grace to the humble."

God isn't asking us to humble ourselves before other people. He's not telling us to humble ourselves before the ways of the world. He's not telling us to somehow drum up humility toward ourselves... He's inviting us to humble ourselves before Him.

If we do that, God promises to shower upon us His favour and kindness. This is an act of *spirit*. It's our spirits that allow us to hear and be empowered by God. We learn to hear God and obey God as we train our souls to be in submission to the spirit/Holy Spirit. The more we pursue the things of the spirit, our souls will desire the things of God. The way we think will change. Our values will evolve. Our desires will take on new and attractive elements. Our ability to make godly choices will open up doors that were previously closed to us. Instead of selfish war being seen as inevitable, selfless love becomes attractive. We consider our loss of standing in other people's eyes as an acceptable cost if only we can live in freedom with Jesus. Our truest identities start to come forward. We begin to love what Jesus loves, and we begin to love people in a way that understands the brokenness of the world while believing that the love of God *never fails* (1 Cor. 13: 8).

Think about this for a minute: God carries within Himself the ability to bring all things into being with nothing more than a thought and word. And it's this same God who promises to shower you with His kindness and favour if you will humble yourself before Him. Does it seem possible that He's able to overcome the war raging in you? Do you think He's able to give you peace and freedom? If you're a follower of Jesus, then your answer to those two questions was probably "Yes, of course God is able to do these things." But maybe the bigger question is this: Does God *want* to do this, and will it actually happen?

Know who you are and live in freedom... let's continue our journey.

CHAPTER 5:

Who Are You?

"A group of Jews was traveling from town to town casting out evil spirits. They tried to use the name of the Lord Jesus in their incantation, saying, 'I command you in the name of Jesus, whom Paul preaches, to come out!' Seven sons of Sceva, a leading priest, were doing this. But one time when they tried it, the evil spirit replied, 'I know Jesus, and I know Paul, but who are you?' Then the man with the evil spirit leaped on them, overpowered them, and attacked them with such violence that they fled from the house, naked and battered" (Acts 19:13–16 NLT).

THERE ARE TIMES WHEN not being recognized can have interesting consequences.

I have a friend who loves to do work on cars in his garage at home. He would often wear those blue coveralls over his clothes to try and keep them clean. One day his wife came home early from work and went into the garage to say hi to her husband. She saw him leaning over into the engine compartment with his back to her, so she went up behind him, gave him a great big hug, snuggled him a bit, then went inside the house. She thought it a little strange that her husband didn't really respond to her when she gave him that loving hug, but didn't think too much about it until she walked into her kitchen and saw her husband standing there! Turns out he had a friend over to help work on the car, and he borrowed his blue coveralls! True story!

Sometimes being unrecognized can have interesting consequences.

Our identity is so very important, and that's why anything that steals or hides it can be so devastating. My mother, who has passed away now, had dementia in the last few years of her life, and though she was still my mom and I loved her deeply, her not knowing who she was or the people around her as well as she once did, certainly changed things. I could feel the distance it created between people, and it changed how we lived with her. We all loved her like crazy, but our deepest connection with her was through our many memories of times when she knew things clearly and we knew her clearly as well. It was from the times of genuine *knowing* that gave us our deepest connections.

Identity Matters

Jesus walked among people in ancient Israel and did things that really got him noticed. He wasn't trying to become famous or seeking a spotlight, but He was all-in when it came to doing everything His heavenly Father wanted Him to do. And this stirred things up!

He taught people how to address the things that were really at the bottom of their struggles, and this often meant casting out demons from people that were being harassed and held in prisons of pain, because of the demon's presence. But there were also some people who didn't identify with Jesus who tried to do these things as well. What I mean is there were some who had heard about Him, were trying to do the same things as He did (like casting out demons), but didn't really find their identity in Him. And this had some pretty serious consequences...

It says in Acts 19:13–16 that there were Jews who were going around "driving out evil spirits" from people. At first glance this sounds like a good thing. If Jesus was casting out demons from people in order that they be set free, then others doing the same thing seems great all around. But it wasn't great for anyone in this account...

These Jews were trying to cast out demons *using* Jesus' name to do so. And again, at first glance, this might sound alright. After all, Jesus Himself taught His disciples in John 14:13–14 NIV that He would do anything they ask for when they ask for it in His name. "And I will do whatever you ask in my name, so that the Father may be glorified in the Son. You may ask me for anything in my name, and I will do it." So what's the problem if there were some Jews doing the exact thing Jesus said?

It has to do with *identity*. Just listen to what the demon said to the seven sons of Sceva when they tried to cast it out using Jesus' name: "I know Jesus, and I know Paul, but who are you?" (Acts 19:15 NLT) Some versions have the demon saying that he knows Jesus and knows "about" Paul, but the use of the Greek words here means that the demon has firsthand knowledge of Jesus and has no firsthand experience of Paul, just that he knows *of* him. Regardless, these two people are *known* by the demon. This knowledge carries with it some kind of important element that translates into *power*. Jesus cast out demons with a word, so did Paul, and both of these men find their identity in relation to God. For Jesus it was a relationship with the Father and empowered by the Holy Spirit. For Paul it was a relationship with Jesus and the Father and empowered by the Holy Spirit. But the seven sons of Sceva *are not known*. They are unrecognized by demonic forces. And because they are unrecognized, they are beaten to a pulp.

Their lack of identity in Jesus prevents them from accomplishing God's work. They try to *use* the name of Jesus to do the work, but that is not sufficient. The missing piece here is that their identity is not found in Jesus, and it renders them unrecognizable and without spiritual power.

The Presence of God Is Key

The seven sons of Sceva lacked identity, so the demon did not recognize them nor their attempt to cast him out. The presence of God within them was not there, and the presence of God is the key. Wherever God goes things change.

When Jesus showed up to address Paul (Saul at the time) who was travelling on his horse to Damascus, Paul was thrown down and was blinded.

God's presence changes things!

When the Holy Spirit visited the people gathered in the upper room, they were filled with power to transform the world.

God's presence changes things!

When heavenly Father comes down upon Mt. Sinai and the people of Israel experience His awesome presence; they could do nothing but tremble.

God's presence changes things!

And God's presence changes people's identities as well...

In Exodus 32 we read about how the people of God (Israel) had committed idolatry by worshipping a golden calf instead of the Living God. This was like the straw that broke the camel's back to God. He had given Israel freedom from slavery and was bringing them into a beautiful and bountiful land where they would flourish, and they simply abandoned Him for a dead idol.

God was not pleased. And so in chapter 33 the Lord has a dialogue with Moses. God said that He was sending the people into the land, but He would not go with them because of His anger toward them. Instead, He would send a powerful angel to go with them who would drive out all of God's enemies from the land. But Moses knew that if God didn't go with them, it would have devastating consequences. This is what he said to God in Exodus 33:16 NLT: "How will anyone know that you look favourably on me–on me and on your people–if you don't go with us? For your presence among us sets your people and me apart from all other people on the earth."

Did you pick up on that? If God's *presence* doesn't go with Israel, then they would be *unrecognizable* to others. That's exactly what happened to the seven sons of Sceva; they were unrecognizable to the demon because God's presence wasn't with them.

And so we have established from Scripture that God's presence provides *identity* to His people. But we haven't yet established why it is that so many of God's people today don't seem to really know who they are in Christ? It can seem that many of us operate like the seven sons of Sceva. We can pray and ask for things in Jesus' name, but nothing seems to happen. Why is that? We even have the presence of God within us through the Holy Spirit, and yet we struggle to know who we are in Him. We can also feel like we identify with non-Christians just as much as we do with Christians. How does this make any sense at all?

Well, one thing we need to do is understand what is really going on spiritually. What is it that was won for us by Jesus' sacrifice? What have we been given? What do we do with what we have been given? And finally, what role does our identity in Christ play in all of this? At the end of it all, my belief is that you will not only have more clarity of understanding who you are, but you will also be in a position to experience freedom that might be very new to you!

We continue our journey...

CHAPTER 6:

Understanding Your True Identity

"The mind governed by the flesh is death, but the mind governed by the Spirit is life and peace. The mind governed by the flesh is hostile to God; it does not submit to God's law nor can it do so. Those who are in the realm of the flesh cannot please God. You, however, are not in the realm of the flesh but are in the realm of the Spirit, if indeed the Spirit of God lives in you" (Romans 8: 6–11 NIV).

RECENTLY I HAVE HAD the privilege of joining in prayer with a number of MLAs at the legislative building in Regina, Saskatchewan. I remember the first morning I attended: I walked up the expansive marble steps, entered through the thick oak doors, and had to go through security measures that included having my belongings and even myself scanned thoroughly in order to gain access. Following that procedure, I had to surrender my driver's licence to receive the needed visitor's pass, and then finally wait for someone to escort me to the proper office where we met to pray.

All of this contributed to a sense of being involved in something very important. It would be true to say that because this was new to me, my experience was heightened. But it's still true to say that I felt it was genuinely important to be involved in approaching God for His presence and power to be invited to come and provide real influence in a place of governance. This is a place where decisions are made that have real impact on people's lives and to be a part of that made an impression on me. I honour those who continue to govern by humbling themselves before God and asking that He would be the ultimate Influencer over not only the decisions and policies being forged, but also over the people of the great province of Saskatchewan.

Governing is a very interesting thing, especially in a democratic society. It's interesting because it provides a real opportunity for each individual to participate in the governing process. Every person has opinions about their lives and the greater societal frameworks they live within. Their opinions influence those around them, and in turn, those individuals are influenced by others. All this contributes to a place of having a sense or feel about it. A significant influencing factor in the creation of the feel of a society is what the government thinks and does. Governments, like individual people, have personalities. They have a way of engaging, and the decisions they make are born out of a way of thinking, a worldview, if you will. If a government has as its primary mandate (stated or unstated) to have better government, then it will marshal its resources in a way to enhance its self-existence. Indirectly this could be a good thing for the people, but is more likely to create a self-preservationist government that looks out for itself before the people it's meant to govern. I think that a government that is motivated by, and holds overtly to, a mandate to exist for the people first and foremost, will provide governance that is willing to sacrifice in order to contribute to the overall good of its people.

Governance matters greatly.

And governance matters greatly when it comes to understanding our identity in Christ.

Why do I say that? Well, one of the reasons this is so important is because of the influences I find in the West. One of the highest values held within our western democracies is the idea of the self-created individual. I mean self-created in that we hold the decisions that we make as the means by which we build our lives. If we make decisions that allow us to build wealth, for example, then we celebrate those who have created for themselves the capacity to retire and enjoy the last third of their lives in relative ease. The important thing I want you to remember here is the idea that our choices are often seen as the most important thing. Make wise choices, reap good rewards.

If you combine the idea of the self-created person based on their choices with the idea of the *individual* who is making those choices, then we enhance our understanding of what is highly valued in our western societies. Much like we highly value choices, we also highly value *the individual* making those choices. Individuality allows for easily identifiable judgments. It is a lot harder to justify financial rewards for someone if the wealth created was built by everyone. Who is it that should be allocated the wealth? However, if an individual is the centre of attention, and that person has accomplished something, then to allocate (and celebrate) rewards to that individual is much easier.

Individuality has built within it something else that's not as easily identifiable but is very important in understanding our identity in Christ. You see, individuality bifurcates things; it divides and sections off in order to make sense of itself. Instead of a whole, you think in terms of parts, and this translates into a way of thinking when it comes to trying to understand who you really are. Here is what I mean...

People's identities can't easily be boiled down to individual components of time. We are the composites of a myriad of experiences and influences that have shaped and moulded us in more ways than we can really imagine. We have been influenced by parents and family, even before we were able to string sensible thoughts together in our infancy. We have been a part of innumerable experiences through our adolescent relationships, and the good and bad things that have taken place have coloured our way of seeing our world. The consequence of all these influences has caused us to see ourselves in a certain way as well.

OK, so where does that leave us? So far what I'm saying is that our identities have been formed within a culture that highly values individuals who make individual choices. We recognize that our lives are more than just a string of individual choices, but the only way we can really judge whether choices are good or bad is to judge them one by one. And so we then elevate the value of each individual choice. You will see the importance of this very soon...

The reason it's important for us to get a handle on how our culture has taught us to value things like individuality, choice, and responsibility is because these things bleed into our understanding of ourselves. If I have described, with any accuracy, how we have been taught just how valuable choices are to each individual, then this exalted value will exert influence into and upon the things that apply to my identity. If I have been trained to see myself as the sum of *my* choices (individual responsibility), then to have someone say that my identity is now somehow defined by, or tied to, someone else becomes incredibly difficult to accept.

The apostle Paul says this in Galatians 2:20 NIV: "I have been crucified with Christ and I no longer live, but Christ lives in me. The life I now live in the body, I live by faith in the Son of God, who loved me and gave himself for me." How hard it is for our souls to accept this truth! It's no longer my thinking that makes my life move forward but Christ's thinking in me. It's no longer my choices that define my life's path but Christ's choices in me. It's no longer my feelings that paint my soul but the feelings of Christ in me. It's now *His* life that is my life. *He* is now responsible for me. All the ways that my culture has taught me to survive by elevating the importance of my choices and my individuality are now crucified on the cross, and it's up to God to guide me. This might sound a bit hard to accept. After all, we do have wills that are designed by God to make choices. That's true, but for a disciple of Jesus, the reality is that our choices must submit to His first.

Maybe it becomes a bit clearer to see how challenging it is for my soul to submit to God. It's only through submission to His Spirit that I will find, and experience, the freedom that's already embedded in my spirit through the indwelling Spirit of God. If my soul refuses to accept this, then I will live divided and separated from God's freedom in my experience. This is a huge challenge because my soul is going to find it difficult to be convinced of the rationality of the decision to submit to the guidance of God's Spirit. Why? Because it's foolishness to a worldly trained mind. Our minds are in a deceived position whenever they operate apart from the Spirit.

We don't actually have the capacity to choose when we operate in the spirit or in the soul. We *always* operate out of our souls, it's only a matter of whether our souls are submitted to the spirit or simply operating on its own. I think you can see that whenever our souls try to operate on their own, they are operating based on the sin-influenced things of this world and will not be able to function in freedom. It's all or nothing. We either submit to God's Spirit, humbling ourselves in order to put our souls under this authority, or not. I think you can see that if our souls have been trained by our culture to elevate our own will (choices), and rationality (mind), and that is seen and understood as taking responsibility, that to shift that responsibility onto someone else who is claiming responsibility *for* us, is pretty difficult to overcome. It doesn't seem like an interesting alternative; it feels irresponsible. And this reality greatly hinders our experience of freedom in our relationship with God.

Governance and Identity

I want to take you back to Romans 8 for a moment. In verse 6 it says, "The mind governed by the flesh is death, but the mind governed by the Spirit is life and peace." We see Paul talking here about *governance*, and this is really important for us to get right.

Governance has a characteristic that makes it bigger than the individual and the choices of that individual. It's tied to something on a much larger scale. When a political party is elected to govern, then it has been elevated to a status that's more than just singular choices that are made within the legislative building. Let me try to explain... We must remember that there are other parties that have a presence within the building, making choices that are often at odds with the governing party. So if the non-governing party presents a budget item that's in direct opposition to the governing one, does that mean that governance has changed? Not at all. Once governance is established, the ruling party obtains a ruling status that is stable, even among opposing opinions.

Now let's bring this down to the individual level. Where I live (in the province of Saskatchewan in the great nation of Canada) the elected party affirms the laws of the land, and this would include something as simple as traffic laws. Now imagine that I'm having a particularly bad day, and I let my frustration out by driving recklessly. In my anger, I choose to cut people off, and my aggressive driving catches the attention of the police who promptly pull me over and give me a ticket, which I rightly deserve.

I have made an individual choice to drive as I see fit, which happens to be in opposition to the governing party's policies that uphold the laws of the land. The question I want to ask you is this: have my choices changed who is governing me? Has my individually chosen path caused me to somehow come out from under the governing authority that has been placed over me?

Obviously not.

But if this is true, then I want you to consider verses 6–9 of chapter 8 in Romans. Here it talks of governance, of what is currently the overarching dictating authority. This authority stands above individual choices, though individual choices still have consequences. It says: "...the mind governed by the Spirit is life and peace" (NIV). Then it makes the association of governing with the idea of being "in the realm of." Verse 8 says that "Those who are in the realm of the flesh cannot please God." This means that a person who is being governed by sinful flesh is living in the realm being overseen by the flesh. This is talking about a person who is not saved and is not governed by Christ.

Now, if we continue to verse 9, we begin to see how this idea of governance affects our identities. It says, "You, however, are not in the realm of the flesh but are in the realm of the Spirit, if indeed the Spirit of God lives in you." A person who has accepted Christ as Saviour is governed by the Spirit of God, and that person lives in that realm.

Now, when that person makes a decision to do something sinful, does that change who is governing them? If you make an individual choice that leads to sin, like I did in my car to drive recklessly, does that mean that you have now overwhelmed the governing authorities?

Here is a key that cannot be overestimated in importance: *Your identity is not tied to your ongoing individual choices because the only determining factor of your identity is who is governing you.* Verse 9 of chapter 8 in Romans says this: "You, however, are not in the realm of the flesh but are in the realm of the Spirit, if indeed the Spirit of God lives in you."

Is It in You?

In the early 2000s Gatorade came out with a slogan entitled "Is it in you?" It showed high level athletes training hard to achieve their goals and that if they used Gatorade, their bodies would be able to go the distance and find success. If Gatorade was in them, they would find what they were looking for.

We should ask a similar question when it comes to our identities in Jesus Christ. Are our identities tied to our individual choices, or are they tied to something far bigger? Does it have more to do with what I choose or who is in me?

It would seem that God is saying to us in Romans 8:9 that if His Holy Spirit resides within us, then we are His, and when we are His, that means we have been given a brand new identity and are under His authority and governance.

This doesn't mean that we won't still struggle. As a matter of fact, the very next verse following verse 9 affirms that the struggle is real. Verse 10 says, "But if Christ is in you, then even though your body is subject to death because of sin, the Spirit gives life because of righteousness." Sin is in our sphere, and where sin is, death is also. We will still experience the miseries that accompany sin until our time on earth is done, but that doesn't mean that we are not in a magnificent process of overcoming, and living out, our new identity in Christ now!

Future and Now

Paul says in Romans 8:18 NIV, "I consider that our present sufferings are not worth comparing with the glory that will be revealed in us."

Think about that for a minute: We are found in Christ, and we still experience suffering. The Enemy wants to use every moment of suffering to try and prove to you that you're disqualified to be in Christ. This is just not true! Suffering will happen. Sometimes it will happen because of outside circumstances, and sometimes they will arise from within you, but it still doesn't change who is *governing you*. The Spirit lives within you, and you will still experience some struggles. But if you keep your Spirit-empowered mind focused on Jesus, you will overcome the lies of the Enemy and experience increasing peace, joy, and freedom!

Paul goes on in Romans 8:31 to verify this when he says that in light of all these things that have been revealed to him by God, what should we make of it? "If God is for us, then who can be against us?" In this present time, we will experience some suffering, but we will also experience increased freedom in Christ. No one can be against us. Not the devil, not our enemies, *not even myself*, because the only version of myself that tries to convince me that my individual choice has somehow threatened my identity in Christ that's cemented in the reality of the presence of the Holy Spirit living in me, watching over me, and governing me is a lie based on my *false self*. My false self is where I live when I allow my focus to be on the flesh and worldliness. A key for living in freedom in Christ is to know that my sinful flesh is still actively involved in my soul that tries to assert itself over my spirit which has been made alive by the Spirit of God living within me. When the struggle with sin is real, and we are feeling the despair or frustration associated with that, we reorient and put our focus back on Jesus, back on the Holy Spirit within us, back on our truest identity that has been set in stone by God Himself.

I think we need to take a breath here and just settle a bit. We have learned that our identities in Christ are tied more to the governing presence of the Holy Spirit living within us than it is about ongoing individual choices. Our choices still matter, but they have more to do with how we live and experience freedom in Jesus, than it does with who we actually are. It can become overwhelming to really absorb this, and there is much we need to still explore. But let the final thought of this chapter be your comfort...

Paul concludes chapter 8 with this incredible truth: "...in all these things we are more than conquerors through him who loves us." The Greek word used for "conquerors" is *hupernikao*, which translates into English as "prevailing mightily." So, when you sin and have become influenced by the devil who tries to convince you that you have forfeited your identity in Christ Jesus, the Spirit of God within you, who gives you your identity and your strength, causes you to *prevail mightily*. You still belong! When you experience the miseries of sin in the broken world around you, you *prevail mightily* because the Holy Spirit is still governing you. And it's true to say that *you* prevail mightily because the Bible describes the real you as the one found in Christ. Paul sees things from God's perspective, and what He sees is stable and strong. It might feel like you are losing, but that's only because you're experiencing things through your sinful soul (more on that later). Your identity is *not* found in your struggling soul. It's found in your spirit where the Holy Spirit now lives.

There is nothing that can separate you from the love Jesus has for you. The Father is absolutely in accord with this because He's responsible for sending Jesus to come and save you. The Holy Spirit is one hundred percent all-in with love for you because He participates in the same Godhead that is committed to pouring out His divine love over you and into you. And by the way, this love is way more than just a feeling; it's powerfully transforming and *never fails* (1 Cor. 13:8).

And it won't fail you...

CHAPTER 7:

Your True and Your False Identity

"Both the one who makes people holy and those who are made holy are of the same family. So Jesus is not ashamed to call them brothers and sisters" (Hebrews 2:11 NIV).

"If the part of the dough offered as firstfruits is holy, then the whole batch is holy; if the root is holy, so are the branches" (Romans 11:16 NIV).

I HAVEN'T LIVED IN the world of horses, so I don't claim to be an equine expert by any stretch of the imagination. But over the years you pick up on things, and I've picked up a few thoughts about horses and how they are valued.

I was six years old when Secretariat won the Triple Crown in 1973. I also remember that this was no average racehorse. This stallion *decimated* his competitors, and because it was such a high-stakes sport, there were a lot of people interested in who this horse was and what he could do.

I did a little looking around, and discovered that the semen of successful racehorses is incredibly valuable. In fact, it might be the most expensive liquid found on earth! Some estimates of current highly successful racehorses can fetch up to *49 million dollars per gallon!*[1]

Now the question that arises from this little tidbit of information is this: *why is this important to the discussion of our identity in Jesus*? And the answer would be that *where you come from matters.*

The value of Secretariat's semen was based on his strength and his successful record. He had a pedigree that allowed him to rise to the top, dominating all the other horses of his time. And people knew that what was in Secretariat would be passed on to those who were born of him. I think you can see where I'm going with this...

In Hebrews 2:11 we read something important about what happened when we were born again into Jesus. It says that Jesus has the capacity to make people holy, and it goes on to say that He actually does make people holy. When He does this, it accomplishes the amazing feat of creating a new family. Both the One who "makes people holy" and those who are "made holy" are of the same "family". The Greek word used for family here is *adelphos* which comes from "alpha," which means "the beginning or starting point," and "delphus," which means "womb." So what Jesus accomplished when he saved us was to begin in us a brand new birth. This birth was from *His* lineage. What made Him, now makes us, *us*. If Jesus was Holy, then we are also holy... the same family.

People who knew the horse world knew that Secretariat's semen would produce a lineage that would very likely contain

---

[1] "The World's Most Expensive Liquid", Standardbred Canada, April 17, 2020, https://standardbredcanada.ca/news/4-17-20/worlds-most-expensive-liquid.html.

similar character traits as he did. This meant immense potential for racing success. The offspring of Secretariat would likely inherit the strength, speed, and temperament of their father who exhibited such incredible traits.

Even though I am using Secretariat as an example to help us understand our new identities in Jesus, it would be false of me to suggest the offspring of Secretariat and the offspring of Jesus receive *exactly* the same thing. The reason it would be false is that the owners of Secretariat's offspring knew that there was only a chance of similar traits being passed down, no guarantees. And that's not at all what is being communicated to us as the offspring of God through Jesus!

We are not being called *similar* to Jesus. In fact, we are being called *the same* as Jesus! Because Jesus is holy, then we are holy as well. The term used for holy in this passage is *hagiazo*, which means "to make holy," "to treat as holy," "set apart as holy," "hallowed." When our lives are made new in Jesus, God then considers us as holy and treats us as such. When God looks upon us, He sees the mantle of Jesus upon us and considers us as set apart from the world. God's view of us is that in Jesus, we are now considered *hallowed*.

Hallowed comes up in another place in Scripture. In Matthew 6 we find the disciples of Jesus wanting to be like Him and not knowing how to do that. They had seen Him go and pray in a way that was so different from the religious leaders of the day. It was as though Jesus was standing there right in the presence of God Himself whenever He prayed, and they were intrigued. And so they asked Jesus one day if He would teach them how to pray. We find the beginning of His response in Matthew 6:9: "This, then, is how you should pray: 'Our Father in heaven, hallowed be your name...'"

The Greek word used here to describe the name of God is the same as the one used to describe us in Hebrews 2:11. Both mean holy. We have been made new. We have been made holy because Jesus is holy, and He has given us a new identity. We have been brought out of a womb into a brand new life of holiness. Our new lineage is as a part of the same family in which Jesus participates.

Romans 11:16 talks of this same reality, but with different language. Here it says that whatever is in a batch of dough is entirely contained within each part. So if you were to cut off a portion of the dough, it would have the same characteristics as the rest of the remaining batch. Jesus is considered the "firstfruits" of this batch. And what is the batch being described here? It's the new family being produced through Jesus' sacrificial life now found in people who have put their faith in Him. He is considered by God as the holy original portion and then goes on to consider the whole batch as holy. That, my friend, is you and I. We have been made new and holy in Jesus.

This is our identity. This is who we have become. But wait! A better way to say this is to say that this is *who we have been made*. I like this better because to use the word "become" allows a little bit of a thought that suggests that I have had something to do with this incredible new life, and I haven't. No. I have not become holy; I have been made holy through Jesus.

New Things

Near the end of time as we know it, we hear God emphatically declare what He has desired to do throughout all human history. He says in Revelation 21:5 "I am making everything new!" And then He tells John (the apostle who was receiving this revelation) to "Write this down, for these words are trustworthy and true."

God is committed to making all things new. He restates the importance of this, and He only does that when He's trying very hard to emphasize something. We can know that it's a value of God to renew and restore that which He created. What He made perfect, that became defaced and lost, is something that is on His radar to address.

God is in the business of making things new.

So then consider 2 Corinthians 5:17: "Therefore, if anyone is in Christ, the new creation has come: The old has gone, the new is here!"

Anyone who has said yes to Jesus as their Saviour has experienced the gift of a new creation. The old has been taken away and the new *is* here. It *is* here. It *is* in you. In fact it *is* you!

I remember growing up on the farm; one of the yearly tasks was to bale hay for feed so the cows could eat during the winter months. We had this old Oliver baler that had issues with its tying mechanism. It was designed so a pick-up would lift the hay on the ground, bringing it into a chamber, where a plunger would push the hay into a compacted form. Once enough hay was pushed into this chamber, a tying mechanism would be triggered encircling the string around the bale and when tied it would hold the bale together.

At least that's how it was *supposed* to work.

It seemed that the part of the machine responsible for tying the bale string would take a vacation about every ten bales, and we would have to stop, manually tie the strings, and then off we would go again. This sequence would happen again and again, until there were more dints in the side of the baler from frustrated kicks than there were bales in the field!

I also remember when we got a *new* baler. It was a New Holland brand and was quite a bit of an upgrade over that old Oliver. It seemed to have a better sense of its responsibilities, so when it came time to tie the string, it actually did its job. The new was far superior to the old.

The same is true for us when it comes to our identity in Christ. The new life that has been given to us in Jesus is far superior to the old life that it replaced. It has all the character traits of Jesus.

All of His goodness, strength, power, character, life, love, and freedom that He enjoys now lives within us. That's the reality that has been given to us in this new life.

God Desires to Bless His Children

I have an amazing dad. He's the most patient and self-sacrificing man I know. When I was young, I might not have had the language to describe it, but in hindsight, I know that my dad wanted to bless me. The same is true of our heavenly Father.

In James 1:17 we see clearly the heart of God toward His children when we read: "Every good and perfect gift is from above, coming down from the Father of the heavenly lights, who does not change like shifting shadows." And Matthew 7:11 says, "If you, then, though you are evil, know how to give good gifts to your children, how much more will your Father in heaven give good gifts to those who ask him!"

And if we ever harbour doubts about Jesus and His attitude toward us, this passage should help us to get a solid grip on just how in agreement with the heavenly Father He is. This is what it says in John 10:10b: "I have come that they may have life, and have it to the full."

Good gifts come from God to His children. Perfect gifts that bring joy are lavished upon God's kids. Life that's bursting at the seams with blessing is poured out over God's offspring. He loves His family and desires that they experience the fullness of what life is meant to be.

This is something the Enemy tries very hard to distort. He takes the idea of a full life and tries to convince us this happens with the best and newest stuff, like houses, cars, trips and bank accounts. Satan takes God's idea of heavenly originated blessing and makes it into a worldly one. The end result is that people then miss out on the fullness of life as God designed it because they have been convinced that God is not really a part of it.

Christians can fall into this trap as well. We adopt a view of spiritual life that puts relationship with God into small categories of religious service, but then struggle to understand why they experience so much frustration in their walk as Christians. They believe in Jesus as their Saviour, but they don't have much of an understanding of what it means to be a disciple of Jesus, except for a belief that being a disciple means forfeiting all the really good things this world can provide.

The fullness of life that Jesus promises to His brothers and sisters starts with an understanding that God is truly good; that each person who has put their trust in Jesus has been given a brand new identity as a whole new creation; and that God desires that each one of His children would *experience* the reality of their new identity in Him.

This is where the experience of freedom comes into play that we will talk about in coming chapters. God gives us new identities in Jesus, and His desire is that we experience the effects of these new identities as well. But for many of the people of God, there is a huge gap between their new identity in Christ and their experience of that new identity. We most definitely want to explore that further!

For now, though, we need to continue on our journey of growing in our understanding of our identities. We have talked about the identity that we have been given: we *are* holy because Jesus is holy and that has been infused into us; and in our new identities we are blessed by God who gives all the good and perfect gifts that He desires to lavish on His children. This is the reality within us in our spirit. But our *souls* are still a battleground, and this is where Satan does his work to try and convince us of false identities that rob us of so much blessing and freedom.

Our False Identities

Let's go back to John 10:10. The second half of this verse is where Jesus tells us that He is committed to giving to His family a life that is full of blessing. But the first half of this verse tells a very different story. It says in John 10:10a: "The thief comes only to steal and kill and destroy..."

The thief here is Satan. Jesus describes him as the one whose primary purpose is to steal the blessings that are meant to be enjoyed by God's children. He steals them away, and if he can't steal them, he will try to kill them by convincing people that what God says isn't really true and then point people to the brokenness of the world and the pain that people experience as proof that he's right. He tries to convince God's children that God isn't really good, and isn't really good toward His children because if He was, then they wouldn't experience so much pain and loss.

If Satan can't outright steal God's blessings, or entirely kill them as described above, then he will destroy them. He will taint them or try to colour them a little bit off so they lose their intent and purpose. He sows a little bit of evil into an otherwise good thing in order to make it something that it's not meant to be.

Have you ever been at a church service that was so filled with God's presence that it was palpable? His manifest presence was so strong that you experienced the fullness of God? And then at the end of the service you come across a brother in Christ who starts complaining about the music or the message or about another brother or sister, and this bit of complaining evil infects the blessing that you had just experienced moments earlier?

Satan will use anything at his disposal in order to *steal* God's blessing, *kill* God's blessing, or *destroy* God's blessing. He can't do anything else because it's so deeply ingrained in him. In fact, Jesus backs me up in this statement. Go back again to John 10:10:

Jesus says that the "thief" (Satan) comes *only* to steal, kill and destroy. It's the only thing he knows how to do.

If Satan offers you something good, it always has an expiration date, and it always leads to pain and suffering. If he provides you an open door for a job promotion, but it isn't something that God had in mind for you, then it will lead you down a path toward desiring more worldly things. If the Enemy arranges for someone of authority to give you a word of praise, then it will be tainted with pride and vanity which will lead you toward selfishness instead of selflessness.

Everything the Enemy desires for you is the opposite of what God desires for you. It's really difficult to see sometimes, and that's why God's grace is so incredible because He's committed to teaching us the differences between the seemingly good things the thief offers, and the genuinely good the Father and Jesus offer.

And this is true in something as fundamental as our identities.

Living in Our Souls

Our souls are incredible in their capacity to help us engage in the world around us. We describe them as having three elements: mind, emotion, and will. Each has a specific function, and they do their roles extremely well. In Genesis 1 we read about God bringing into being a variety of created things—light, stars, planets, vegetation, land, sea and air creatures—and after He created each new thing He called it "good." The Hebrew word used here is *towb* which means "beautiful," "pleasant," "agreeable." This was the response God had when He saw what He had made.

Then He wanted to outdo Himself! He created human beings, who were the creatures who would most closely resemble Him. They would bear His image, carrying elements very similar to God that no other creature was given. The blessing and honour

He bestowed on humans was simply astounding. And God knew just how incredible these image bearers were. We know this because after He created us, He says in Genesis 1:31 that we were *meod towb* or <u>very</u> good. *Meod* means "abundantly." So what God made in human beings is now not just beautiful, pleasant, and agreeable, but *abundantly* beautiful and *abundantly* pleasant and *abundantly* agreeable.

Please take a moment to let this sink in... What God put within human beings moved Him to joy and deep appreciation. To Him, man and woman are abundantly good. This has never changed. He has always retained this clear-sighted and deeply-held conviction that what He created in man and woman is abundantly good. Does that seem hard to accept given that He has taken steps to punish and sometimes to kill people who were living disobediently toward Him?

We read in Genesis 6:5 NASB the devastating effects that sin had on the world after Adam and Eve chose to pursue their own agendas instead of honouring God's will for their lives. This introduction of sin into the created order was horrifically destructive. This is what it says in verse 5: "Then the Lord saw that the wickedness of man was great on the earth, and that every intent of the thoughts of his heart was only evil continually."

But, as I said before, God never lost sight of the abundantly good image bearers that He had made. And this is depicted so clearly when we are given an inside look at God's own heart... He was filled with *grief* that He had made these reflections of Himself and that they had fallen so very far. The Aramaic word for grief here is *atsab*, which means to hurt, to have pain. God's own heart was filled with pain as He saw His own children living as they were not meant to be.

So why am I telling you all of this? What does this have to do with our identities? Well, as it turns out, quite a lot actually.

When God first made Adam and Eve, he made the prototypical human beings. They were made perfectly. God made them with a spirit that was designed to be the mechanism through which they would commune with God. Their spirits were to be the ruling element that would be directly connected to God Himself. To be clear, Adam and Eve's spirits did not make them divine (having the nature of God), but it is where God's divine presence could commune with them directly, giving them life.

They were also made abundantly good in their souls. This is where their minds, emotions, and wills resided and served under the authority of their spirit. Because their souls were sinless, they had no trouble in allowing their minds to submit to the guidance of God's Spirit and wisdom. Their emotions were also under the authority of the spirit as was their capacity to choose (the exercising of their will). The soul was the bridge between the spiritual world and the physical world. The guidance provided by the Spirit of God would be received by their souls, and this is where the mind, emotion, and will would process and apply the spiritual guidance into the physical world around them.

When Adam and Eve sinned, this perfect order was ruined. Sin caused the spiritual part of these abundantly good image bearers to die. No longer was communion with God seamless. Now it was up to the soul to try and figure things out. The soul was never meant to be the tool for direct communion with God, and since it was now cut off from the Spirit of God, it could only process the information it gathered from the physical world it found itself in. There were hints of God, memories of God, but as those memories faded, the souls of humanity wandered further and further away until all that was left were evil intents described in Genesis 6:5.

Again, it says in that passage that every intent of the "thoughts of the heart was only evil continually." The Aramaic word for "heart" used here is *leb*, which describes the inner man, the mind, the will. Though it doesn't mention emotions, it is describing the *soul* of the human being. In essence it's describing the journey from Adam and Eve, who had thriving spirits communing with God openly and perfectly, receiving life and direction that their souls could apply to their physical lives, to now humanity having access to only their souls that have been cut off from the Spirit, which led to their souls having nothing but evil intents all the time.

This reminds me of Romans 8:7–8 NASB that says: "...the mind set on the flesh is hostile toward God; for it does not subject itself to the law of God, for it is not even able to do so; and those who are in the flesh cannot please God."

When the spirit of a human being dies due to sin, the soul is cut off from spirit access. The soul's mind then can only be focused on what it has access to, and that is the natural world and everything that is in it. One of the primary things that affects the natural world is sin, and so sin, then, is a continual driver and influencer of the soul's mind. Because sin, by its nature, is rebellious toward God, a soul's mind that is cut off from Spirit becomes corrupted by sin, and it can no longer subject itself to the authority of God. *It cannot do so.* To be clear, this means that the soul has no power or capacity to engage in godly things, whether overt or subtle, and simply does not have within itself the ability to please God.

When the spirit of a person dies, the inevitable result is that the soul has no way of re-engaging in a communal relationship with God and His Spirit that brings life and guidance to the soul.

The Importance of Jesus

We can begin to see just how important the original design of humanity was! God made the first man and woman abundantly good. God never lost sight of that incredible reality and was grieved in His heart when people became deceived and were cut off from the Spirit that was so essential for life. The impossibility of reconnecting with God led Him to an extreme solution: He would send His own Son to bear His image in the flesh in sinless perfection again. Jesus would live in the original design that Adam and Eve first enjoyed, but Jesus had a task that Adam and Eve couldn't have accomplished.

He would live a sinless life and represent perfect communion with God but do more than just model it for others to see. He would go much further! Jesus would eventually be *made* sin on our behalf. In 2 Corinthians 5:21 we read, "He made Him who knew no sin to be sin on our behalf, that we might become the righteousness of God in Him."

Do you know what this means?

It means that Jesus took all the sin that infected humanity from the beginning in the garden until today, and because of His sinless life, paid the penalty that sin produces, and that penalty is death. Jesus died sinlessly and took sin to the cross where its power died as well. Jesus didn't just model a life of perfect communion with God, He provided access for people to, once again, experience that life again.

The Original Design Recovered (Sort of...)

When God created Adam and Eve, they enjoyed their perfect design. Their spirits allowed them perfect communion with God, which provided them with supernatural/divine life and guidance. Their souls were untouched by sin and were able to function under the complete authority of their spirits. Their minds were spiritual; their emotions were spiritual, and their wills were spiritual. Equipped with this spiritual power, their souls were able to provide guidance to their bodies which was their vehicle to engage in the natural world around them.

When sin entered the scene, Adam and Eve's souls were cut off from the Spirit's power, life, and guidance and began a process of sinful distancing from God which led to generation after generation wandering away from God and ultimately death.

God was gracious to provide a reprieve from death through the sacrificial system He initiated through the Jewish people and gave them a mandate to reach out to other nations to submit to God. But this was a temporary fix that did not provide access to the original design that God intended for men and women.

That is until Jesus...

Jesus doesn't just cover up people's sins, He destroys sin and its power in those who put their faith in Him. And what's restored is that when a person is forgiven their sin through Jesus, *they are given new life and their spirits are restored within them.* This means that they now have access to what was lost to Adam and Eve in the garden.

Their souls now have access to their spirits and the Spirit of God, once again. The original design is now possible, but is not yet perfected.

Even though we now have our spirits restored within us, and we have been invited into communion with God again through the Holy Spirit, and even though we have been given brand new identities in the Family of God and are called Holy by God Himself, we still have struggles. Those struggles come through a soul that is still wrestling with the effects of sin; one of the biggest challenges is that the soul does not want to submit to God's Spirit. The soul remains rebellious and wants to assert its own authority. This attitude gets translated into very practical things like our minds wanting to figure things out for ourselves. When they read Scripture and God asks us to do something like sell all we have and give it to the poor, we recoil because our soul-led minds simply do not see this as reasonable. In fact, it is seen as irresponsible. This is just one example of *soulish* thinking or the soul still trying to assert its own control instead of submitting to the Spirit's guidance.

We can see this in 1 Corinthians 1:20: "God has made the wisdom of this world look foolish." So even in the minds of believers and followers of Jesus, there is still a battle between our sinless spirits that commune with God and sinful souls that are on a journey of growing in holiness but aren't fully there yet. The original design of spirit ruling soul, and soul submitting to spirit is available but isn't yet complete.

Thankfully, God knows this and gives us ample descriptions in His Word to help on this journey. One of the major things that I hope to highlight in this book is to reveal our true identities in Christ. When we say "yes" to Jesus and give our lives over to Him, He makes us brand new in our spirits. We are now considered holy by God because of Jesus living in us through the Holy Spirit. *But our experience of that identity is often hidden to us because we are still living with dominant souls that have not yet fully submitted to the spirit/Spirit.* This is where our experience of this new identity is hindered. And that's something that I want to address in the next chapter in more detail.

CHAPTER 8:

Our Response to What God Has Done

"Now Christ lives his life in you! And even though your body may be dead because of the effects of sin, his life-giving Spirit imparts life to you because you are fully accepted by God. Yes, God raised Jesus to life! And since God's Spirit of Resurrection lives in you, he will also raise your dying body to life by the same Spirit that breathes life into you! So then, beloved ones, the flesh has no claims on us at all, and we have no further obligation to live in obedience to it. For when you live controlled by the flesh, you are about to die. But if the life of the Spirit puts to death the corrupt ways of the flesh, we then taste his abundant life" (Romans 8:10–12 Passion Translation).

"Therefore, since we are surrounded by such a huge crowd of witnesses to the life of faith, let us strip off every weight that slows us down, especially the sin that so easily trips us up. And let us run with endurance the race God has set before us. We do this by keeping our eyes on Jesus, the champion who initiates and perfects our faith" (Hebrews 12:1–2 NLT).

GROWING UP ON THE farm, you learn a lot about how life works. We were a pretty prototypical operation in that we grew crops and also had a variety of livestock. There were beef cows, and milk cows, along with chickens, turkeys, pigs, and of course, the requisite dogs and cats (the latter were not livestock but pets!).

I remember feeding the pigs. When you poured the feed into the trough, what was a relatively quiet environment turned quickly into chaos! I saw firsthand, in real time, what "survival of the fittest" really means. These pigs were driven by nothing more than instinct and appetite. The biggest and strongest were able to muscle their way to the feed first and were able to stay the longest while they satisfied their hunger. Of course, the smaller ones had to work twice as hard to get their fill as they simply didn't have the strength to bully the bigger ones out of the way.

They all ate, but it was clear that size matters!

It was also clear that these animals had no sense of care or concern for the others in their pen, and this would be true for the biggest *and* the smallest. For all, it was simply a matter of getting what they wanted, and needing to do whatever was necessary to accomplish that goal.

Feeding Desire

There are a lot of similarities between these pigs' desires and the desires that reside within people. Where the pigs lived a simple existence of urges and appetites that didn't go much beyond meeting the needs of their grumbling stomachs, people, though more complicated in nature, still operate with some of these same principles.

I have a sense that in the following lines I will be treading on thin ice, and I want to ensure that I communicate the dignity and respect that every human being deserves. I have just talked about the basic instincts that drive animals to act based on their desires and appetites. And now I'm speaking of similar traits in people. This can seem demeaning, and that isn't my intent whatsoever. But it's true that people have instincts and appetites that get expressed as desires, and if these desires arise from a place of brokenness apart from God, then they can have pretty devastating results. In fact, it can take people down desperate roads that seem as though there is little hope. When we see people in these dark places, it can be easy to judge them and give trite words that have no power to heal but only condemn. Again, that is not my intent nor is it my heart. But we must look at the reality of what sin can do and how it affects the desires that drive us. Please keep that in mind as you consider the following...

Have you ever seen someone who seems to choose to pursue something in their life that when they actually get what they want, it provides only frustration and loss? Let me give you an example:

I remember visiting East Hastings Street in Vancouver a number of years ago. This infamous street is known for the vast numbers of people who have fallen victim to alcohol or drug use. The street is covered with cardboard boxes that serve as people's homes. There are small tents that are filled with people's belongings. There are sleeping bags all over the place and garbage seems to be everywhere. People are standing, sitting, and laying on the sidewalks and on the streets. One thing I remember clearly is that the lives of these people did not remain on the sidewalks, but spilled out onto the streets. It just seemed to me to be an example of how the borders of life didn't seem to apply here for these dear ones who had lost their way.

It's impossible for me to know all the different ways, influences, injustices, inflictions, and injurious events that had led them to be there on the street, but one thing was clear, and that was that they were *there*. They were real, and they were in an incredibly tough place, an impossible place.

It wasn't hard to understand that the pain that they had endured, the pain that somehow touched a place so deep in them that the only way it seemed they could ever experience a tiny bit of light was to put chemicals into their bodies so they could escape, for even a short and fleeting time, *made sense*. Given their circumstances, it was deemed reasonable to gain a short reprieve knowing that the long-term effects would be even more devastating for them.

It would be so unfair to simply say that they were succumbing to their desires, and that if they would simply wake up, drum up some courage and discipline, then they could put themselves on a better road. This way of looking at them is naive and doesn't reflect an accurate understanding of their journey.

But it would also be incorrect to say that they are making choices not based on their desires because at the most fundamental level that is exactly what they are doing, *just as we all do*. All people make choices based on what they desire, even when those desires lead us to accept things into our lives that hurt or even destroy us.

In my own natural and fleshly desires I operate in just the same way. This is what happens when my soul comes out from under the authority of my spirit and the Spirit of God. I seek after what I desire. When I say that, I am reminded that we always seek after our desires; it's just a matter of whether they are spiritual desires that line up with God or they are natural/worldly desires that are guided by our sinful and broken world.

The Brutality of the Soul-Led Person

Growing up in the church has been an overall blessing to me. I have learned so much about who God is and have experienced His presence there time and time again. Unfortunately, I have also seen and experienced some watering down of God's message through my time in the church. One way this happens is when we talk of sin and its devastating effects on people.

There really is no way to talk about sin, really describe it accurately, and then somehow pretty it up. We sometimes use different terms to describe sin in our attempts to soften the blunt impact of what sin does. We use "slip ups" instead of sin; we talk of "mistakes" or "tendencies" all with the intent to make it sound a little more palatable. And I think we often have good intent in not wanting to hurt people we care about, but really we do more damage than good by not allowing sin to be just that... sin. Sometimes it's the best thing for us to realize the weight of what sin is and what it does.

When we become soul-led people, apart from the spirit-led design that God originally intended for us, we find ourselves allowing sin to influence us and our desires. The Bible has strong words that describe for us what sin really does, and we need to hear that clearly.

James 4:1–2 explains that when our desires are not godly, we will choose to walk on paths that bring destruction. We have "desires that battle within," which is to say that our soul-led selves create war zones inside of us. We respond to these battles by embracing our desires that arise from them, and this leads to fights, quarrels, and even death. We begin to lose all sense of God and His ways, and we covet what other people have and feel slighted when we don't get what we think we deserve. So we reach out with a desperate cry to God, calling to Him to give us what we want, but this falls on deaf ears, because God knows that we are screaming for action to satisfy our selfish/soulish desires.

And the real crazy thing is this: *We keep on doing this again and again!* We pursue what our desires want and rail against God who seems to have forgotten about us. So our fallen reason then justifies going even harder for the things our souls long for because, at least, it will give us some kind of reward even if God won't bend to our desires.

We might think this is a fit description for broken people who have fallen into drug addiction, but the same is true for the ones who have fallen into work habits that require them to be on task eighty hours a week. They have adopted a view that this is the only way to get to that place where they have a nice house and two or three cars and the ability to go on a nice vacation each year. It doesn't matter that they have zero time and energy for family or for God, because what they are pursuing is what they *desire* even though it's killing them. They likely wouldn't even say that they desire this lifestyle, but that they don't see any other way out. You see, they have been taught that this is the only way to live. They have been taught that the good life requires these things from them. The only problem is that even when they get what they are pursuing, it doesn't bring satisfaction. But they keep on doing the same things even though it's killing them.

Sounds pretty similar to what happens on East Hastings Street, doesn't it?

You Empower What You Choose to Focus On

God sees just how much sin has affected us. It blinds us to see our own destructive behaviours driven by our desires. It's literally a prison that holds us in bondage. And that's why Jesus' sacrifice for us is so important. His perfect sacrifice breaks the power of sin and allows us to see clearly what's really going on. He provides for us the ability to choose a different path when we simply could not do that before He came onto the scene of our lives.

But Jesus also knows that even though we have been given a new life and a new identity in Him when we accepted Him as our Saviour, we are still in a battle to experience the freedom He wants for us.

James 4:7–10 NIV says, "Submit yourselves, then, to God. Resist the devil, and he will flee from you. Come near to God and he will come near to you. Wash your hands, you sinners, and purify your hearts, you double-minded. Grieve, mourn and wail. Change your laughter to mourning and your joy to gloom. Humble yourselves before the Lord, and he will lift you up."

Submission requires acknowledging that your current agenda needs to be given up for someone else's agenda. To submit is to accept the authority of another's way. This is incredibly hard for our souls to do because in their worldly way of thinking, submission is weakness, and that's the last thing it wants to do.

We justify not submitting, in so many ways, in our world. We're always talking about advocating for ourselves in a system that's trying to take us down. We talk about standing up for our rights in a world that's bent on pouring out injustice upon us. We elevate our heroes who have stood against all the odds, and have risen above the rest, because they simply refused to *submit*.

No. We don't like the idea of submitting. It's seen as a weakness and is so often perceived as an embarrassing lack of character.

Is it possible that this way of thinking and living is not much different than how those pigs act when the feed is poured into their trough? Does this not sound much like a survival of the fittest mentality? Is there not something in us that simply would rather lift ourselves up instead of submitting in order for someone else to lift us up?

And yet God calls His children to a different way of living than what the world values.

"Humble yourselves before the Lord and he will lift you up."

Sounds great until you actually submit and humble yourself before God while everyone else around you (Christians often included) are still living according to the code of the world that says, "It's all on you, so live strong and fight hard to get what you want and need."

You are judged as one who has given up and has lost.

No one said it would be easy to live according to God's ways in a broken world. No one guaranteed that when you said "yes" to Jesus and became alive in your spirit that your soul would immediately follow suit. Followers of Christ not only have to fight the battles around them, but also *within* them! But the benefits of fighting this good fight, learning how to submit to God, and living according to the Spirit is a treasure that's beyond compare. Sounds good maybe, but is there a way to begin to understand how to move forward in all this? The short answer is "yes," and it starts with learning the following principle: *what you focus on is what you empower.* This has immense implications for our experience of freedom in Christ that we will see shortly.

If you've ever played hockey, you'll know that it's tricky to score a goal on a really good goaltender. You give him your best shots, and sometimes scoring can seem nearly impossible. Of course, you're trying to get the puck *past* him, and that means that you aim away from his body. But as you do that you get closer and closer to the posts on either side of him. If you struggle long enough to score, you begin to not only look past the goalie, but *at* the post. When you start looking at the post, it is likely that you'll shoot the puck right at it, which, of course, ends up not accomplishing the goal at all! If you look at the post, you'll hit it more often than not.

In this example, what you're focusing on becomes larger and larger until it consumes your vision. You started out with a clear vision of scoring goals, of hitting the netting behind the goalie, but that was displaced by a goalie that got in your way. You were taken off your original vision, and your attention was diverted. To get away from the goalie your attention was then attracted to the post, which ended in failure as well. It became more about *avoiding* challenges instead of *achieving* the original vision or goal... hitting the back of the net with that puck. This analogy demonstrates that what you focus on is what you end up empowering, and it consumes your vision and your pursuits. The same is true in our spiritual walk with Jesus.

Romans 8:12 tells us that since we have the Spirit of Jesus living within us, we are no longer obligated to live according to the natural, worldly ways of thinking. We are not bound to live in obedience to the flesh or the broken sinful ways we are so familiar with. But not being obligated does not mean that we will automatically find ourselves experiencing freedom. It just means that we now have the ability to choose what our path will be.

Obedience can take place in one of two ways: it can happen through force or through invitation. If someone is stronger than me and threatens to hurt me if I don't do what they want, then I am being forced against my will. But if someone is stronger than me and offers to use their strength to help me if I agree to join with them, then I am being invited not forced.

This is exactly what's going on in Romans 8:12. In this world there is a powerful Enemy who has threatened harm to people for generations. He exerts force through sin and all the tools associated with sin, and traps people into believing all sorts of ungodly and life-destroying lies. In this place of forced obedience, the devil convinces us to do our best to use our souls (thinking, emotions, and will) to navigate life all the while condemning us for failing every step of the way. Without the guidance of the Spirit, we have no hope of ever coming out from under that reality.

But when Jesus comes onto the scene, He exerts a different kind of power. He breaks apart the strength of the Enemy and all of his lies. He sets all the captives to this deception free, and then He gives each of them a new life and a new identity. But as wonderful as this is within a person's spirit, the soul remains in the battlefield of struggle with sin. The soul is still fighting to retain dominance and finds it very difficult to give up control.

Now remember that our soul is where we experience life. It's the place of awareness, and all of our lives are lived there. Everything we are talking about in terms of experiencing freedom takes place within our souls, where all of our thinking, all of our feelings, and all of our choices take place. Our world of experience takes place within our souls, so when we talk about our *reality*, how we think, feel, and act toward others, toward ourselves, and toward God, we are talking about our souls. This is a big deal.

God made our souls to exist in freedom *only* under the authority of His Spirit living within us. Romans 8 tells us that we have been given a new identity in our revived spirits, and that we are no longer obligated to serve sin. However, this doesn't automatically mean that we will *experience* the freedom that comes with these identities. We still have choices to make.

We must choose where our focus will be. If our souls still choose to rely on worldly thinking, while not being intentionally submitted to God, then our experience of freedom will be far, far less. If my feelings are still focused and responding primarily to what comes from the world around me, instead of my feelings being focused on the Holy Spirit first, then my experience of freedom will be greatly reduced. If I still make choices and exercise my will based on the way life works around me, instead of being submitted intentionally to the Holy Spirit, then I will be robbed of experiencing freedom. *What we focus on, we empower and what we empower, we experience.* Focus on God's Spirit in us, and our souls will experience freedom. Focus on the world's ways, and our souls will experience bondage.

Our *identities* are still found in Jesus, but our *experience of freedom that comes from those identities* are dependent on where our focus is. Because every soul still struggles to submit to God's Spirit and authority, every soul experiences an amount of floundering and hindered freedom. The truest freedom that Jesus desires for His children then *feels* distant, and we lose sight of the incredible experience of freedom in Him.

So Jesus does something about this situation. He invites us to see and accept that our souls can grow in freedom as well! He tells us things like Romans 8:12, that we are no longer under any obligation to live in the lies that held us in bondage for years. He says that we can choose to submit to the Spirit within us and by doing so we will be lifted up into a new experience of freedom that is just waiting to be unfurled in our minds, emotions, and wills.

But this is an *invitation* and must be something that we choose and embrace. Choosing seems like it should be such a simple thing to do, but it often isn't because we almost always choose what we desire, and our souls still desire things that are not of God.

Our souls don't easily see the glory and goodness of God residing within our spirits. They have a very difficult time perceiving the reality of our new identities in Christ. It's clear to God that we have new identities in Him, but our thoughts, feelings, and choices often convince us of a very different story.

We are told that as believers in Christ we have been given freedom and life, and it all sounds wonderful, and we have times when we actually believe it to be true, but then someone hacks into my bank and steals my money, and I get distracted by all the pain and loss, and my soul becomes focused on the brokenness of this world and all that I need to do to overcome it in my own strength (because no one is going to do it for me, right?). In that place of distraction, I lose sight of the glory of Jesus and how He desires to meet my needs. I lose sight of my true identity in Christ and focus on my false identity... the one that I create through my struggling soul by my own choices, thoughts, and feelings. I get focused on the goalie or the goalposts and lose sight of the fact that living in Jesus is like taking the perfect slapshot and hitting nothing but net!

A Great Alternative

It's amazing to experience being saved. Now, when I say "saved" here, I'm not talking about when Jesus forgave my sins and became my Saviour. What I mean is something that is a little more of a daily living kind of thing.

I remember a few years ago, an example of how this happened to me. I was pastoring Strasbourg Alliance Church in Strasbourg, Saskatchewan. A little town just outside of the capital city, Regina. My church was filled with good people and good leaders who knew Jesus and knew how to model the good things that come from Him in real and practical ways.

Even though these were really good people and God was pouring out blessing, there were still times of challenge and stress, and I was going through one of those times. It got to the point where my body responded to the stress by having a seizure that knocked me out and blanked out my memory for forty-eight hours. Turns out that this started a chain of events that would alter the course of my life (again!).

When I experienced that seizure, I fell and hit my head on the floor. We didn't know it at the time, but this started bleeding to occur on both hemispheres of my brain. Over the course of the next few weeks I started to have severe headaches, my balance started to be affected, and it was getting increasingly difficult to walk. We went into the hospital and found out the extent of the bleeding was severe to say the least. It was only a matter of a day or two and the surgeon had drilled burr holes in my skull and inserted tubes to relieve the pressure on my brain by draining all the excess blood that had pooled there.

We were told that it was potentially only a matter of days and I could have died. But the Lord had different plans!

As I said before, I was pastoring a church of people who loved Jesus and knew how to model a life of blessing... And they showed me and my wife just how much this is true.

For a couple of years I had been wrestling with a call from the Lord regarding a change of ministry direction and had felt led to submit my resignation to my board. I had just submitted this when all of the brain bleeding issues took place. My board saw fit to suspend my resignation in order to access the needed medical funding that insurance would provide. They took it upon themselves to navigate the frustrating process of dealing with claims and on top of it all, put on their shoulders the added responsibilities to cover all the areas that were left unattended due to my absence. My board and particularly my staff really stepped up!

If I could summarize all of this, they saved me. They took what they had learned from Jesus about life and service and applied it directly to me and my wife. As I write this I feel such a deep gratitude toward them for their sacrifice and care. They didn't get distracted by the brokenness of the situation and kept their eyes on Jesus. They could have let frustration cause them to hesitate or limit how much they would do for me, but they didn't. The facts of the circumstances couldn't shake them from keeping their eyes on Jesus and His incredible favour and blessing... and it flowed through them to me.

Do you know what this kind of focus accomplished? *Freedom.* By keeping their eyes on Jesus, I was given freedom. I had the time I needed to heal and to find my path again. I had the provision that allowed me to follow the Lord's leading in my life. And that blessing continues to this day.

I share this with you as a great example of an alternative that is presented to us every day as followers of Jesus. Our souls take hits all the time. We make decisions that don't pan out like we had hoped, and we experience hurt and loss. We lose money on an investment that seemed solid; we feel the pain of someone's harsh words; we experience severe confusion when we thought we had something figured out when it took an unexpected turn and caused doubt to arise. And then on top of it all, the Enemy gets his licks in by heaping guilt, shame, condemnation and a whole list of life stealing things onto us, and all that I have described conspires to distract us enough onto ourselves so we lose sight of Jesus. We become so soul focused that we lose sight of the Spirit who desires to lead and support us.

And when that happens we *experience* what we are looking at. Instead of experiencing the reality of the identity we have been given in Christ with all the benefits and blessings that come with that, we experience the reality of the pain, frustration, and loss because our focus has been drawn to our circumstances, and that's all we can see.

If we do this for enough years, we then learn to cope. If our focus is on our souls, and their tools (thinking, emotion, and will), and we don't allow them to be submitted intentionally and daily to the Spirit, we learn how to cope with our circumstances as best we know how. We rely on *our* thinking to figure out a way through. We depend on *our* feelings to determine what is happening in our relationships. We lean on *our* will to strengthen us to walk the path through difficult life circumstances. And we convince ourselves that this is the only way we can live. We tell ourselves that we are being responsible by carrying all the loads that get heaped on us. And then we have moments where we realize that it seems like Jesus is a million miles away... We ask ourselves if this is all that life in Him really is. And because it seems like it can't be any other way, we then convince ourselves that life with Jesus now is little more than a test of endurance in order to get to the good stuff after we die.

I want to say this as gently, and yet as emphatically, as I possibly can: *This is a lie.* Jesus brings salvation and new identity in Him so that His children would *experience* life in Him. He came in order to pour *abundantly* into His family. Jesus came to sacrifice and pour Himself *out* in order that He could be poured *in* to each one who would put their trust in Him. He came in order to give life, that people who had the courage to say "yes" to Him would be *filled*... a new identity in spirit and a new *experience* of His love in soul.

There is a great alternative to having our focus on our hurts, pains, challenges, and worldly things that our souls try to navigate on their own every day. It's to begin to see that submitting to the spirit within you, where the Spirit of God resides and desires to pour into you, shape you, and lift you up above your circumstances, is the place of experience of the goodness of God that is designed for *you*.

Jesus is calling each one of us to get our eyes off our false identities that we build up through lifetimes of self-thought, self-emotion, and self-will. They are false when we lean on them apart from submission to the Spirit of God. This is trying to live independently of God. His presence in us is not meant to assure us only of eternal life with Him in the future, but instead is meant to be the presence that guides every part of us, every single day. Our souls may see this as a burden and confusing because they have not yet fully learned how to submit. It doesn't make sense to us how to accomplish this. That's simply the reality of an exalted soulish life that has not yet learned how to submit to the Spirit. And that can change.

As we step into the God-ordained, original plan and make-up of humanity, we will begin to experience an increase of freedom. This freedom will begin to shape us and how we think. We will begin to see the wisdom of heaven as making more sense than how we previously thought about how to engage our world and circumstances. We will begin to feel the things that Jesus feels. Instead of being wracked with jealousy or self-doubt or anger, we'll begin to feel peaceful when we simply couldn't before.

Why? Because we are putting our focus on Jesus and the Holy Spirit. This causes us to experience the things of God right here and right now. We'll begin to see our ability to choose things of God instead of things of this world more easily and readily. We'll begin to recognize a shift in us: where it was difficult to choose to make time to be with God in His Word, we will begin to see a longing to be with Him there.

Everything that resides in God resides in us because God resides in us. He is the most peace-filled, joy experiencing, confidence inspiring Being in all existence. *And He lives in us.*

You might question some of the things I am writing here, but I think you would have to admit that the more that we find our lives in God, the more we will experience the things of God.

After all, He really is good.

The Best Cheering Section Ever

I remember going to a hockey game with my soon-to-be-wife. She got tickets given to her in the season tickets holding section at Northlands Coliseum in Edmonton, Alberta. It was in the 80s when the Oilers were the singular dominant force in the league. Needless to say the section we were sitting in were rabid fans!

For some reason I got this crazy idea in my head to cheer for the other team. If I remember correctly, it was the Philadelphia Flyers who were playing against Wayne Gretzky and Co.

Every time Philadelphia would score, I would scream my approval. Every time the ref called a Philly penalty, I would loudly express my disapproval. As I said, I don't really know why I did this, but I did.

I remember yelling for yet another Philadelphia goal, and this was the last straw for a little old lady who was sitting right in front of us. She slowly stood up, turned around, and while looking straight at me, proceeded to firmly and confidently express her opinion of me and concluded by emphatically telling me to "shut up!" Needless to say, I was not sitting in a section that was cheering for me! But we do have a cheering section in heaven that is genuinely pulling for us.

It says in Hebrews 12:1 that we are surrounded by a huge crowd of witnesses. These are people described as people of great faith, who have overcome the challenges of this world and have experienced God's faithfulness in their lives. They *see us*, you and I. Our names are written in the Book of Life, right alongside theirs, and they're literally cheering us on.

It says in 11:39–40 that they lived for God, but they didn't yet receive "all that God had promised. For God had something better in mind for us, so that they would not reach perfection without us." I think this means that God had in mind that He was going to bring in the full number of people who He wanted to experience life with Him, and these people who are in heaven know that we are those that make up the rest of those numbers *and they are cheering us on in order to make it all the way*!

They are cheering us toward the finish line. But it's not just about getting to the finish line of life. God has in mind for us to live as *more than conquerors*. He's inviting us to experience the fullness of His life in us even now. We will still need to endure suffering, brokenness, and loss... Jesus Himself had to go through that. But God's plan for His children, His church, is to live in the fullness of life in Him, against all the odds, and in the midst of our incredibly obvious weaknesses.

We are *surrounded* by a great cloud of witnesses cheering us to step into life so that the world would see Jesus shining through us in ways that confound the world and worldly thinking. And we are called to join in this journey. So how do we do that?

We are to "strip off every weight that slows us down, especially the sin that so easily trips us up" (12:1). Our souls take on sin every time we try to live according to our own wisdom and strength. But this great cloud of cheering witnesses is calling out to us to humble ourselves and confess our sins so that our souls would be clean and able to turn and submit to the Spirit who pours more and more life into our minds, emotions, and will. These witnesses are standing in the season ticket holding section of the world, and are unashamedly yelling to us their approval for every victory we experience, and they are courageously and loudly urging us to overcome when we fall, pointing us back to Jesus so we will live in freedom and shine hope to the world around us. They are unafraid when the Enemy stands up and tells them to shut up! They don't shrink back because they see the finish line so very clearly. They are the voices, who in agreement with God say to us, "We are for you and not against you!"

We are being called to run this race and not give up. In fact, Jesus is calling us to run an even *higher* race! An impossible one! One that requires giving up on our strength, which seems crazy if we think about it. Who gives up their strength when they're facing a huge and challenging race? Only those who are called to depend on a greater strength in order to accomplish the tasks that can only be accomplished through the One who calls us.

How do we run this impossible race? Oh man, I am so filled with joy right now... ! God has laid out the plan in plain sight. The Enemy sees it, and God has tipped His hand. It's the most exhilarating thing imaginable when your opponent knows what you're going to do to win, and then you do exactly that, but they're still *powerless* to stop you. If you want to join in with this great cloud of witnesses and follow Jesus into a life of increasing freedom where the glory of God shines in you and through you, regardless of the opposition that arises around you, then do this; listen to the words and the plan of God for your life of freedom. "We do this by keeping our eyes on Jesus, the champion who initiates and perfects our faith" (Hebrews 12:2 NLT).

Keep your eyes on the prize. Don't look at the goalie or the post or the pain or the hurt or to your own thoughts, strength, feelings, or will. When you do this, you bleed out your freedom. Keep your eyes on the prize, the goal, and that's to live in the freedom that's already in you by the Spirit of God through Jesus... *Keep your eyes on Jesus.* Do this and you will win more than you could have ever imagined.

CHAPTER 9:

What God Does

"But while he was still a long way off, his father saw him and was filled with compassion for him; he ran to his son, threw his arms around him and kissed him" (Luke 15:20 NIV).

IN THE LAST CHAPTER I did a lot of talking about winning against the odds, and against strong opponents that are trying to defeat you, and against the sin that puts pressure on you from without and within. Jesus calls you to keep your eyes on Him and your identity in Him will translate into freedom in your experience of Him. This is entirely appropriate as it is a high value and goal of God for His kids.

But we need to recognize that there will be times when we just fall short. We'll sometimes fail to keep our eyes on Jesus and our gaze will wander onto what sin offers instead. We are in the midst of a battle for our souls that is very real and is imminently present. This would be incredibly bad news for us if our identities in Christ were up for grabs every time we sinned. We would be in a state of perpetual anxiety, never being sure if our last sin disqualified us for good.

I have said previously that it does us no good to soft-pedal sin. It's brutal, beastly, and downright *bad*. When our still fallen souls embrace what sin offers, we soon realize that we have, once again, poured a toxic mess onto our minds, our emotions, and our wills. It not only confuses us, but it opens the door to condemnation, shame, and self-destructive behaviour. It's not something that we should mess around with.

We have to be vigilant to understand and agree with everything the Bible teaches us, and one important thing is that sin is still something with which we struggle. In 1 John 1:8 we are told that "If we claim to be without sin the truth is not in us." I have spent a lot of time explaining that when we receive Jesus as our Saviour we are given a brand new identity in Him that is holy and made clean. This is the reality of our *spirit*, and we are confident that this identity in Jesus is solid. This is where our true nature resides, and it's where we are to look for strength, guidance, hope, and light in order to live as followers of Jesus.

But in our *souls* we still wrestle with sin. This is where 1 John 1:8 comes into play. If we say that we have a new identity in Christ and that we are saved and holy, then we need to understand that this is not referring to our souls. Our spiritual identity in Jesus is holy and pure, and our soulish reality is that we still wrestle with sin. And this is such a big deal to understand because it's in our souls that we experience all of life here on earth. It's not hard to imagine, then, that if your whole existence, and experience of that existence, is still immersed in and fighting with sin, that it would be easy to see *yourself* that way too, that is to see your identity as a sinful person. But we need to remember that God says that with Jesus now in you, you *are holy*. It's so easy to allow all those thoughts of condemnation that accuse you because of how your soul embraced sin, as evidence that you really aren't holy at all. It's easy to fall into the idea that you are inevitably and irretrievably broken. But that's where we need to put on the brakes!

Paul said in Romans 7:20, "Now if I do what I do not want to do, it is no longer I who do it, but it is sin living in me that does it." It's imperative that we remember that when we sin, and it's something that we know is wrong, even though its attraction is too great in the moment and so we embrace it and act on it, *it is not an action that is coming from my truest and solid identity, but it is a reality of something that still has a place within my make-up that exerts influence.* It isn't "I" that does it but sin in me.

Even as I write this truth I find my soul rebelling against the idea. My experience has taught me that if I do something then I should take responsibility for that action. If the words come out of my mouth, then what I said falls on me, good or bad. If my hands perform an action, then the consequences of that action should fall on me. If I make a choice, then the fallout from that choice is mine and mine alone. The world holds me accountable, and that makes sense to me.

But then what about what Paul says in Romans 7:20? It seems as though he *isn't* being held responsible for his actions in some significant way. And maybe this is opening the door for us to understand the very real-world implications of what Jesus accomplished for us on the cross. Isn't it true that because of sin *I* deserve to die? And isn't it also true that Jesus died *on my behalf* so that I wouldn't die in my sin? And isn't it right to say that Jesus died because of sin *even though He committed no sin at all*? So it seems that the reality of the kingdom of God is to accomplish the pouring out of blessing that is not deserved through sacrifice from someone who doesn't deserve punishment at all.

Seems kind of upside down, doesn't it?

So maybe it actually *is* true that when Paul sins, he knows that his soul has committed something that deserves punishment and *will* receive punishment from the world. Even though his true identity of holiness in his spirit is established, his soul is still not yet fully redeemed. One day it will be set entirely free, it's just not there yet.

We Still Live in This World

Colossians 3 really gives us some insights about being both holy and sinful at the same time. Those that have put their trust in Jesus have been "raised with Christ" (3:1). This is something that has already taken place. This is talking about our spiritual reality, where our true identity resides. But then this is immediately followed by the admonition in verse 2 to "Set your minds on things above, not on earthly things." We are seated in the heavenlies with Christ, but we are still wrestling with earthly things, and we are commanded to make sure that we are *choosing* to focus on heavenly/spiritual things. We choose with our wills, which is found in our souls. This is an invitation to submit our souls under the authority and guidance of our spirit and the Holy Spirit that lives with us there.

It goes on in verse 3 to say that we have *died* and that our lives are now hidden with Christ in God. If we are dead and yet are considered alive, then we need to understand what this really means. Our spirits were dead before Jesus raised them to life. Our life is now secured through Jesus in God. It required death to sin in order to be raised to life. But then in verse 5 it says that we should "put to death, therefore, whatever belongs to your earthly nature..." If you look at the Greek phrasing for this verse, it says that our earthly nature is literally the *members which are upon the earth*. And this makes total sense...

Remember that we have already died and have been raised to life in Christ, and we are seated with Him in the heavenly realms (Ephesians 2:6). In this, our *spirits* have been made alive. But we also know that as human beings we have been made with spirits and *souls and bodies*. The soul is to be the tool through which the interpretation of spiritual things takes place in order for it to exercise authority and instruct the body what to do. The soul and the body are our *earthly* tools. So we are told in Colossians 3 that we are to put to death whatever belongs to our *earthly nature* that's telling us that we are to take our souls and our bodies and submit them to the authority and guidance of the Holy Spirit in order to be trained in righteous living. And to live righteously is to live in true *freedom!*

Learning New Rules for Living

It's easy to underestimate what it really means to live your whole life through the lenses of your soul. All of your thinking takes place there. Every thought you have is produced through the exercising of your rational mind. Every single thought you have processed arises from here. The very foundation of your lived experience has emerged through decades of experience.

Every feeling you have experienced, the way you react when someone speaks a critical word that hits a place of weakness and vulnerability in you and gives rise to emotional responses, happens within your soul. Every sense of exhilaration that bubbles up when you do something that excites you or brings you joy has been produced in your soul.

The multitudes of experiences that have taught you about the choices you have made in the past, the choices you are facing now, and the implications of choices that have future impact in your life are all constructed within your soul.

Now add these together. Your thinking is influenced by your emotional response to some things that transfer into what choices you make. Past conversations flavour not only what you think but also how you feel about those thoughts and the potential actions you may choose to launch into. All of your thoughts, feelings, and choices, both potential and actual, all feed into one another to create an overall sense of your world view.

There is nothing in your current world view that you do not look through in order to interpret your reality. It's entirely comprehensive to you. This is where you have lived for your whole life. The sheer magnitude of data that has been processed by you to get you to where you stand today is beyond calculating. You, indeed, have been fearfully and wonderfully made!

Now please consider that this comprehensive totality that has created for you your understanding of every single thing that you currently understand, from the most minute and seemingly insignificant detail, to the grandest theory that you can imagine, *has been affected by sin at least on some level.* Sin's greatest tool is to deceive, and to cause false conclusions that lead to pathways that point away from God.

Do you see just how devastating sin is and how it affects every aspect of your soul?

We have learned how life works in this life. I know that sounds silly and almost naive, but it's still true. *This* world of existence is where we were taught how things work. It's here that I have learned that if I do something, then I am wholly responsible for the consequences, and I have learned that it would simply be wrong for me to think that someone else should take responsibility for something that I have done.

In this world, I have learned that my "I," my identity, is tied to what my soul and body do. This earthly existence is amazing but incredibly limited. It simply doesn't have the tools necessary to comprehend a whole different life that is predicated on *spirit* and the principles that reside in the spiritual realm.

So when Paul says that when he sins it is no longer he that does it, he is revealing his understanding that his true identity, the *foundation* of who he now really is, is no longer found in his soul-mind/thinking, or his soul-emotion/feelings, or his soul-will/choices, but is now found in the *spirit*/Holy Spirit/ Jesus. He is recognizing that there is a different reality that dictates what actually is. He sees Jesus as his identity as his spirit has now been set free to live in Him empowered by the Holy Spirit. He sees that even though he is wrestling with sin and sometimes even chooses it, this is not being done from his new spiritual identity that comes from God.

It's like we are being asked to consider Hebrews 11:1 that says, "Now faith is the assurance of things hoped for, the conviction of things not seen" (NASB). Paul, being convicted, knows that his true identity is found in Jesus and in the Spirit of God. He can't see that he is seated with Jesus in heaven, but he knows that it's true. He sees that he still wrestles with sin, and can experience the evidence of his actions with his own physical eyes, but he's confident that when God says that he's holy because Jesus has made him holy, that this is absolutely right.

The challenge for you and I is to see ourselves the same way. Do you know that if you have given your life to Jesus, that the most solid and true aspect of you is now found in your spirit? Do you know that you can experience the freedom that comes with this identity? The more we submit our souls to our spirits, the more that freedom will rise up in us.

Holding It All Together

Remember that all the life you live is lived out of your soul. It's through your soul-mind that you engage in conversation with other people. If your soul is wracked with uncontrolled sin, it will have a huge impact on what you reflect to other people. It's God's desire that you reflect His Son so that others may know Him and be saved and set free. The soul is the bridge that communicates what the Spirit desires to express. The same is true for our emotions: if our souls are so beat up and desensitized by sinful things, then our emotions will be all over the map, and it will be incredibly difficult to be open to empathize with others who are hurting and searching for answers. Again, not the goal that God had in mind for you as His child. And finally, if your soul is being bombarded with sin, it will cause your will, that is your ability to make decisions, to become much more self-oriented and much less other-oriented. This will hinder your ability to order your life in such a way that it becomes an invitation for others to find health, life, goodness, and ultimately, Jesus Himself.

Now because our lived experience takes place within our souls, if they are immersed in uncontrolled and unopposed sin, it will blind us to who *we* really are in Christ. We end up living a lie, and we become even more open to the lies of the Enemy because we're hindered from receiving the truth and power we need from the Spirit that resides within us. If we are living in our false identities, then our freedom is incredibly diminished, and we end up walking in our own mess and trying to make it through life leaning on our abilities instead of being guided and strengthened by the Spirit of God who desires us to experience the fullness of life that God imagined for us all along.

Yes, sin in the soul is a massively big deal. But I want to remind you that one of the main goals of this book is to help you in experiencing increased freedom in *you*. That matters to God because He genuinely loves you and freedom is one of the most beautiful byproducts of true love. This is so important for us to remember, and when I say "remember" I mean much deeper than simple cognitive recall. I'm talking about getting this truth into our *bones*. Why? Because we sin, and when we do, it hurts like crazy. It disorients us and sometimes makes it nearly impossible to think straight. In truth, we need help. This is where our incredibly good God steps in and shows us how He treats us when we mess up.

Really Understanding Our Father

It's really quite a thing to consider: We have been given the testimony from people of God who have lived over 2000 years ago that's meant to impact our lives *today*. We have been given a book that describes a God who we don't see daily and this book tells us that our lives don't even belong to us but instead to this God. We have been told that this God *loves* us and that we should trust Him with everything we've got. And we've been told that this God is wanting to be our *Father*.

Have I got this right so far?

Now, this Father created the world and everything in it, and it was originally really good. He put people in it, and those people messed it up royally by inviting in a toxic mess that spoils every single thing that this Father created.

Still with me?

Finally, we're invited to believe that this Father also understands that we *continually* mess up even today, and that His desire is to forgive us so we can enjoy a relationship with Him.

Really?

It's very hard to believe that our heavenly Father wants to forgive us when we sin, because we instinctively know that when we do, it really makes a mess. Real people get hurt; actual relationships get broken; we make a mess, and then we continue to live in the mess making it even worse. And we do this to all the things that this Father has made so carefully for us to enjoy. No wonder the Enemy of God is so successful in convincing us that our Heavenly Father is more likely ticked off at us than He is wanting to forgive us.

But that wouldn't be the case that we read about in Luke 15...

A Real-Life Example

The youngest son, in Luke 15, must have been frustrated with his life with his dad. He was stirred up somehow and just wasn't satisfied; he longed for more. The only thing that made sense to him was to get away from where he was, and the only way he could do that was by getting his inheritance early. So he went to his father and asked him for his share of the family estate. The father was likely very hurt by this request, not only because it was essentially telling him that his son thought of him as dead to him (which was a cultural thing of that day as inheritance came *only* after someone died), but it also would have wounded the father's heart because his son simply didn't want to be around him any longer. (This is the power of a soul-led person... and it's brutal).

So the son takes his inheritance, goes far away and lives it up... for a while. When his money runs out, so do his friends, and all he can do is to get a job feeding pigs which doesn't pay the bills or even give him enough to buy food. He finds himself in the gutter, with little hope and no future.

Until he wakes up. There's some little remaining sense within him that maybe his dad will have mercy on him if he will go back to him and beg for forgiveness. He isn't expecting to be fully restored, instead, he will offer to be treated like a hired hand and not a full-on son. To expect that would simply be absurd.

And so the son goes back fully ready with his plan in place, and then the absurd *happens*. We are told that when the son was a long way off in the distance, the father sees him and something amazing takes place: *His heart is filled with compassion for his son.* He sees that his son is making his way home. . and is *immediately* filled with care, love, and concern for him. This feeling was so overwhelming that this mature man, who had built up his business, and had people working for him, and had the respect of many people, caused him to *launch out in a full-on run*. And when he reached his son, he didn't posture himself in a haughty kind of "Hey, I'm waiting for your apology" kind of way. No! He throws his arms around that wayward son and showers love on him with kisses.

This shouldn't have happened because it was simply absurd. But it's only absurd if we think about this whole situation through a soul-led perspective. Through that lens it makes sense that the young boy would try to come back as a slave to his father, because after all, his actions deserve consequences, right? Except for two things:

1. This story is not primarily about what the boy did, but was instead about what the father does.
2. If the boy's choices were to be evidence of what can happen if you are a soul-led person, then we are also given evidence of the sheer power and beauty of what a spirit-led person will do.

And the effects of the former don't stand a chance in the face of the effects of the latter! This father knows what's in his own heart and his actions reflect exactly what's needed in this situation.

(Oh God, fill our souls now with Your Holy Spirit that we too would be just like this father and pour out love and compassion on those around us who from the world's perspective don't deserve it! Fill people with Your Holy Spirit so that when *I* am this lost son and deserve only judgment that I would receive absurd grace!)

And so this wayward son is embraced and kissed by his father, but the wounds go very deep in him, and it seems to kind of just deflect off him. I wouldn't say that the son was immune to his father's shower of love, but he was still pretty soul-focused... He had prepared the requisite repentance speech and offered it promptly to his father, but do you know how the father responded? In verse 21 the son gives his speech and right away in verse 22 we see the father *not even responding to his son's confession and apology.* Instead he immediately calls out to one of his workers to prepare a feast in celebration of the return of his son, and then he calls for a ring to be placed on his finger. Do you know what the significance of this is? It means that the son is being *fully restored into the father's family.*

The father was making a clear statement: "Son, you are forgiven already by simply coming back. You are mine; you have always been mine, and you need to see it and experience it for yourself. My love for you is greater than you can imagine. Welcome. You belong. Be free."

Is It Possible That God's Love for Us Is Much More than We Imagined?

Now I want you to imagine your own situation. You have just committed *that* sin, you know, the one that has dogged you for years. You know the words that Jesus says to his disciples in Matthew 18 when His followers ask him how many times they should forgive a brother or sister for a repeated sinful offence... Jesus says seventy-seven times, meaning, don't stop forgiving them.

Then to illustrate the extremely important nature of this forgiving principle to His disciples, Jesus talks about a servant who was forgiven great debts by his master. After this incredible grace had been given to the servant, he went out and did the very opposite to someone else who had asked for mercy from him. When the master finds out about how his servant abused his freedom, he poured out his fury upon the servant, and placed him in jailers' hands to be tortured and thrown in prison.

And then Jesus says that this is how the heavenly Father will treat each of them (the followers of Jesus) *unless they forgive like the master in the story did.*

Kind of shocking, until you let it sink in for a bit...

Wouldn't it make sense that the principle of this lesson should apply to us in our journey of trying to understand who we really are in Christ and how He wants us to experience freedom?

Let's examine this a bit more. So I fall into a sin, and this is a sin that I have committed repeatedly over the years. Some might call it an addiction, but nevertheless, it's pervasive. I've continually asked the Lord for forgiveness, and I claim His promises in 1 John 1:9 that says if I confess my sins that He's faithful and just to forgive my sins and cleanse me from all righteousness. All good, but I can't help shake this feeling of self-condemnation. I believe in God's promises and put faith in them, but I still heap guilt on myself. Why is that?

It's because my soul has learned that I am supposed to be responsible for my actions and since I have fallen into the same sin, then obviously I haven't learned my lesson. And since my soul lives in a competency based world, and I have proven incompetent and insufficient in my strength, then I deserve all the condemnation that I am experiencing.

I take all of this as a follower of Jesus, recognizing that even though the promises of forgiveness are trustworthy, because my focus is through the lenses of my soul experiences, I must accept this condemnation that is deserved and just tough it out until my time on earth is over, and I will *then* finally be free.

This is not what God is teaching us in the Bible.

Jesus first taught his disciples that the kingdom of God is like a master who forgives debts *when that forgiveness is not deserved.* That should mean something to us. It should tell us that this is a principle of spirit not of soul. And we need to have our souls submitting to the spirit in order to experience the reality of what God desires for us.

"But," you might say, "doesn't the master really let the servant have it when he didn't forgive?" That's true, but it's to teach us something really important. The fact that the master punished the servant was to tell us just how important radical forgiveness really is. Now apply this to yourself: If you have been given a new, free, and holy identity in Christ, and this is how God sees you, and you continue to identify yourself as a sin-filled so-and-so, who deserves self-condemning punishment for repeated sins, then it would seem that you are acting *against* God's perspective of who you really are. Your opinion of yourself is different than God's opinion of you. And anything done in opposition to God is sinful right? Wouldn't that be grounds for asking for forgiveness? *Is it possible that you need to forgive yourself?*

Jesus already said just how important showing mercy and forgiveness is, and when it doesn't happen, then the person is *tortured*. Isn't that exactly what happens when you heap self-condemnation on yourself? You end up living in a lie (not your true God-given identity), opposing God's own view of who you really are in Jesus (seeing yourself through your soul instead of your spirit) and holding onto something that tortures you.

When Paul says that when he sins it isn't really he that is doing it but sin in him, what he's doing is expressing forgiveness toward his soul that hasn't yet learned who he really is yet. But because Paul lives his life experiences through his soul (as every human must) he knows that his soul must submit itself to the spirit and accept the wisdom of God. In this, he aligns himself with God's value system by forgiving himself again and again because that's the radical nature of God's forgiveness toward His kids. He's standing in this radical forgiveness that sets him free, and this allows his soul to thrive in submission to his spirit, and then the light of Jesus shines in and through him. It might seem like he's endorsing sin by letting himself off easy, but that would only be true if one were perceiving Paul through the lens of the soul which has learned the dog-eat-dog mentality of the world. Instead, Paul is exhibiting the perspective of his spirit and the Spirit of God that understands that he and his spirit need to extend forgiveness to his soul that has not yet fully learned the things and ways of God.

Forgiveness sets people free, and forgiving your soul is necessary for you to experience the freedom that your spirit currently enjoys in Jesus. Your soul-mind needs to accept that it must be told what to think by the Spirit and that its own attempt to try and navigate life is futile. Knowledge comes through humility. Your soul-emotions need to accept that they don't have the freedom to feel whatever they want, no matter how justified it might seem, and that it's only in submission to the Spirit that they will be set free to feel what is appropriate. Peace comes through humility. Your soul-will needs to accept that it doesn't have freedom when it makes choices on its own and will only experience freedom when it allows the Spirit of God to teach it what to choose. Right action comes through humility.

I know that our souls fight against this tooth and nail because it just seems so foreign. But this is our reality as children of light that still live in a dark world. Hebrews 11:13 talks about people of great faith in God who are called "foreigners and strangers on earth." They were people who lived according to the Spirit, and that made them conspicuous. It made them stick out like sore thumbs. They were *different* because the world they lived in was soul-led and not spirit-led.

To really begin to get a grip on the reality of our experience is to understand that we have been made alive in our spirit and that this is where our true identity resides according to God's perspective of us, but that it's also true that we live in our souls that fight against the Spirit all the time. In a very real way, we are foreigners to ourselves. What a conundrum!

We need to learn how to live as kingdom-minded followers of Jesus, adhering to the idea, with the tenacity of a pit bull, that we need to forgive our souls for their many and varied shortcomings and sins. We need to learn how to hold on to the importance of knowing just how devastating sin really is, without applying it to our identities in the spirit that have been set free from sin and now live in holiness. We need to learn how to be grace-filled toward our thinking that still finds comfort in darkness; we need to shower forgiveness on our emotions that still pursue unholy desires and find self-pitying pride satisfying; and we need to pour out the love of Jesus on our wills that still stand in rebellion and try to make its own way in its own strength. And we need to overcome the lies of the Enemy that constantly try to keep our eyes on our earthly saturated souls instead of seeing our truest identity in Jesus, and on our place with Him in heaven.

And finally, we need to remember that in the midst of all these challenges, victories and failures, we have a Father who runs after us with seemingly reckless abandon when he sees us walking back to Him. We feel so distant from Him at times, and He runs for us and throws His arms around us and begins to shower love on us. When our souls try to convince us to make sure that we have our proper apologies in place, making sure that we are crossing all the proper religious Ts and dotting all the seemingly important rule-based Is, our Father is already calling out to all those in heaven saying, "Let's celebrate! My son is back!" And when our self-condemnation convinces us to make sure that we pay at least a little bit of the penalty our sin deserves by saying to our heavenly Father, "I know I deserve punishment; just let me have a place among your slaves and that will be enough," our Father puts the ring on our finger that says, "You are part of My family. You belong. You are my son!" And then He gently places a robe on our shoulders and says, "You are a part of My Royalty! And you have access to all of my riches and blessings!"

And then the party begins… Friends, this is exactly how the Father treats you.

CHAPTER 10:

God Is at Work to Set You Free

"Those whom I love I rebuke and discipline. So be earnest and repent. Here I am! I stand at the door and knock. If anyone hears my voice and opens the door, I will come in and eat with that person, and they with me" (Rev. 3:19–20).

"I thank my God every time I remember you. In all my prayers for all of you, I always pray with joy because of your partnership in the gospel from the first day until now, being confident of this, that he who began a good work in you will carry it on to completion until the day of Christ Jesus" (Phil. 1:3–6).

I CAN REMEMBER A time when someone opened a door for me. It's a metaphoric door, but it had real implications in my life to be sure. I had just come out from a pretty challenging ministry situation where my resources were drained and my resolve to serve was fractured and laying strewn on the floor. It was a tough time.

But the Lord showed me such incredible kindness that I couldn't even see at the time. We had just moved to a new town and had begun to serve as the pastor of the church there. It was of a different denomination than I had previously served in and so that meant that I needed to meet with this new district leadership. What followed really impacted me.

I was coming to the table with very little in the tank to offer. In fact, it seemed that I was offering little more than brokenness and hurt. And do you know what this meagre offering was met with? Grace, openness, and acceptance! The whole leadership team welcomed me with open arms even though I was in a season of leaning not leading.

The district superintendent was a man who was striving to lead a spirit-led life and not a soul-led life. He led by trying his very best to listen to the voice of the Holy Spirit, and this produced in him a willingness to do things that sometimes didn't perfectly align with the wisdom of this world. He heard God say to him that he should invite me into a mentoring relationship and that he would like to spend some time with me, and he did. He listened to my flailing soul and provided stabilizing love and guidance that began to bring healing to me.

This man of God opened doors for me that I couldn't even see. He was an instrument of God's grace being poured out when the last thing on my mind was receiving grace-filled gifts of transformation. I was just trying to survive, but my God was not swayed by my broken limitations. Not in the least. Instead, He began the work of prying open blocked doorways that would lead to new revelations of His love. And that's what He tells us about Himself in Revelations 3...

God Opens Doors

I've heard these words from Jesus many, many times. "Here I am! I stand at the door and knock..." These words were accompanied by the picture of Jesus standing at an old wooden door with vines growing all around... all the edges have that fuzzy look implying a romantic feeling of intimacy. I've seen this picture hanging in relatives' homes, in church basements, in books and Bibles. I've heard messages preached on this passage asking people to listen to the voice of Jesus who is calling out for people to be saved. All good things mind you, but I wonder if there is more going on...

Jesus says these words at the very end of a long address to the seven churches of Revelation. He has just finished speaking to the church in Laodicea and then speaks of repentance and His desire to be let in so He can share a feast with those who say "yes" to Him. Given the context of speaking to the churches, doesn't it make sense that He's offering an invitation to those who are already believers in Him? Is it possible that Jesus is asking His followers to allow Him into deeper places in order for Him to show us, and have us experience, the banquet of freedom that He desires for His brothers and sisters to enjoy?

I think so.

I believe this is another example of the audaciously extravagant love of God. He is committed to not only providing for people's salvation, which inaugurates eternal relationship with this God who loves, but also exemplifies His desire to see His children experience the fullness of life through increased freedom here and now. There are doors in the way, but He's committed to opening those doors, so we can share in the banquet.

Jesus is knocking at the doors of our souls. Through His Holy Spirit that's residing within us now, He's inviting us to open ourselves up to Him. He's knocking at the doors of our minds, and asking them to open up to receive wisdom that doesn't come from this world and doesn't make any sense at all unless they are taught a whole new way of thinking. He's knocking at the doors of our emotions and inviting them to give up their anxious tensions that are prone to extreme sensitivities or the flip side of the coin, to deadened desensitization, and exchange this for Spirit-led invigoration that operates on a totally different frame of reference. He's knocking at the door of our wills and inviting them to allow their worldly kingdom defences to be baptized in the blood of Jesus that has already established the heavenly kingdom in our spirits, but is fighting to retain what makes sense to a world-driven will.

God is committed to knocking on doors that hinder our freedom, and He's not stopping. He works when we don't even see it, like when He inspired the district superintendent of the denomination that I had just been introduced to. I was not offering anything of worth except my brokenness, and God worked through my new friend to open a door that would shine in light and hope.

God is committed to His children experiencing increased freedom in Him!

The Unstoppable Love of God

I love using words that excite and motivate. When I try to write something that expresses that kind of enthusiasm, I use exclamation marks to emphasize my point! But to a soul that feels like it's drowning, it usually has the opposite effect. Instead of being filled with strength and energy, the broken soul's response can be deflating and even despairing. There's a faint recognition that what's being said is good, but just enough to justify the feeling that change is impossible because it's so far away. For the Christian who lives in the reality of being soul-led, offers of encouragement can feel like little more than invitations to endurance until this life chapter is over and life on the other side with Jesus arrives.

Except that wouldn't line up with what God actually models for us in Scripture. It was God's own love that motivated the original blessing of life and all the beautiful and wonder-filled delicacies that Adam tasted in the garden. It wouldn't line up with how God opened doors of grace for me when my soul was lost in self-pity, shame, and crushing doubt. It just doesn't line up.

God's love motivates everything He does. It's a part of His nature, and He describes Himself *as* love in 1 John 4:16. I think Paul had times of astonishment when he realized just how powerful and good God's love really was, and I think Phil. 1:6 might have been one of those times...

Paul says in Phil. 1:6 that he is "confident of this, that he who began a good work in you will carry it on to completion until the day of Christ Jesus."

Why was Paul *confident* of this? Wasn't this the man described in Acts 7 as one who was standing watching the stoning of a Christian? Wasn't this the same man who was filled with seething anger, adding his approval as others raised hands that hurled rocks large enough to snuff out a life? Wasn't this the man who watched all of this, confident in his role as a true defender of God, and who was all-in to pursue these so-called believers, dragging them out of their homes and destroying their lives? Why on earth could this man be *confident* that God's love will complete what it starts?

Because Paul was experiencing on a much greater scale, the same things that I was when it seemed like I had come to the end of my resources and yet God was opening doors for me. God was also opening doors for Paul. Even in the midst of his brutal persecution of the people in God's church, God's love was pursuing Him. The same love that motivated Jesus to take on flesh and come to earth, enduring all kinds of insane brutality, in order that people like me and people like Paul might have doors opened for them.

Paul was *confident* that what God starts He also finishes because he had experienced the pursuit of God's relentless love.

It had a massive impact on him; you might say that it led him to become an entirely new man. Hmmm, maybe that's exactly what Paul was remembering when he wrote 2 Corinthians 5:16–19: *"So from now on we regard no one from a worldly point of view. Though we once regarded Christ in this way, we do so no longer. Therefore, if anyone is in Christ, the new creation has come: The old has gone, the new is here! All this is from God, who reconciled us to himself through Christ and gave us the ministry of reconciliation: that God was reconciling the world to himself in Christ, not counting people's sins against them..."*

Paul remembered that he once thought of God from a worldly or soulish perspective. He thought being a follower of God was about rule following and power. He thought it was about establishing righteousness through force, and in the process had built for himself a kingdom of serving that held his soul in a prison of his own making. But Jesus broke through and caused Paul to see something entirely different. He now knew that Jesus had given him a brand new life; an entirely new perspective; a shiny new identity. He knew that God was no longer counting his sins against him and that he was free. He knew this to such a degree that he would even recognize that when he still did fall into sin (in his soul), his new identity in the spirit needed to extend forgiveness to his soul in order to continue the journey of experiencing increased freedom.

You Are Being Offered a New Deal

There used to be a game show on TV called "Let's Make A Deal." A contestant would be given a small prize and then asked if they wanted to risk losing it by choosing another prize that was hidden behind closed doors. They might win big or lose it all, which produced the excitement behind the potential deal.

When you are given a new life in Jesus, you have been given a brand new identity in your spirit, and God wants for you to grow into the fullness of that identity in your soul as well. But your soul is hesitant to fully submit to the spirit because it still wrestles with sin that makes it not only suspicious of this free gift but also tends to be unwilling to accept it at all because it means giving up control. Satan uses these realities to try and convince you that what you need to give up is not worth the new deal being offered to your soul. The ask is too great, and after all, it might end up being nothing more than a booby prize with no value at all.

But Jesus is unwilling to let you fall into the trap of Satan's lies. He's knocking on the door and asking you to let Him and all of His gifts and blessings flow into your soul so that the new deal that has already been given to your spirit in the fullness of identity as a child of God, would flow increasingly into your soul.

Paul was confident that God would complete what He started because he had experienced that increasing freedom flowing from his spirit into his soul. I am blessed to count myself in the same camp as Paul because I am increasingly experiencing freedom in my soul as I submit to the spirit/Spirit. *And the same deal is being presented to you.* Will you allow your thinking, feelings, and choosing to be freed up to experience the freedom found in your already established spirit identity?

God is at work in you to accomplish this already. How do I know this? Because that's the word of encouragement that He speaks through Philippians 2:13 NIV *...for it is God who works in you to will and to act to fulfill his good purpose.* He's already given you an incredible gift of life through Jesus. He's given you a brand spanking new identity in your spirit. All the blessings of God reside in you as the Holy Spirit has taken up residence in you. And He's working in you to help your soul to experience the freedom that your spirit already enjoys. It may seem impossible because your soul has learned deeply rooted ways of coping with sin, but it's not impossible because God says that in Him all things are possible, and you *can do all this through him who gives you strength* (Phil 4:13 NIV). It's a promise you can take to the bank.

He loves when we want to partner with Him just like He offered to Adam when it came to naming the animals in the garden. And He's inviting you to partner with Him now so you can experience freedom like you have never experienced before.

He can do it, and He has made a way for you to do it. It all comes down to this: will you?

At this stage, you may feel exhilaration or desperation, but regardless you are probably asking this question: "But how?" Let's see if we can explore that as we begin to land this plane in the last chapter of our little adventure...

CHAPTER 11:

The Road Forward

"Jesus explained, 'I am the Way, I am the Truth, and I am the Life. No one comes next to the Father except through union with me. To know me is to know my Father too. And from now on you will realize that you have seen him and experienced him'" (John 14:6–7 Passion Translation).

AS A CHILD, I remember when we had some relatives visiting us on our farm in Saskatchewan. I didn't know them well, but it was easy to see that everyone there was enjoying their time together. They were on a bit of a family tour and wanted to also see some other members of the family who lived in another town about two hours away, and I remember they were not sure how to get there. So my dad offered to send me with them to show them the way.

There was only one tiny problem: I didn't know the directions! I'd been to this town a few times before, but you know what it's like when you are a kid and have spent your whole life riding in the back seat... you don't pay attention to directions; you just enjoy reading your comic book and, lo and behold, you show up where you are supposed to be! But Dad was confident that I had what it took and so off I went.

We did pretty well at the beginning, but it soon became clear to me that I had no idea where to tell my relatives to go. It turned out that we did miss an important turn and ended up going a bit further than we should have, and then had to take a gravel road instead of the paved highway to get to our destination, but the miraculous happened, and we made it to where we were going.

Sometimes the road forward is one that we don't expect! Sometimes that road is filled with a lot of doubt and fear. There are times when we just don't have a clue where the next turn is, and it can feel like we're lost, and when it comes to our lives, feeling lost can be pretty brutal. But, more often than not, we end up getting to where we need to be. And that's what I want to stress as we see the checkered flag near the end of this book. I want you to hear that you might feel a bit confused or disoriented when it comes to understanding how your soul and spirit work. You might wonder at how to navigate what it looks like to pursue experiencing increasing freedom by growing into a spirit-led person instead of a soul-led one. So let's see if God provides us with some important but simple to understand ways we can walk on this road toward freedom.

Understanding the Source Matters

When it comes to living in increasing freedom, it's absolutely imperative that we grasp the importance of the source of our freedom. The way that our souls typically function is when we face a problem, it will try to convince us we need to figure out our way forward *on our own*. This is something that we learn right from our very first days on earth... we are to learn how to take care of ourselves. Now a certain aspect of independence is rightly emphasized: it's good that we learn how to leave home and gain knowledge and skill to provide for ourselves and for our families. It's good that we accumulate increased awareness of others' feelings and how to live well with them. And it's important that we learn how to skillfully utilize our wills so that we can make choices that will benefit not only ourselves but also those around us.

But if we remember that all three of the aspects of our souls (mind, emotion, and will) are affected by sin then it should make us pause when it comes to figuring out how to live in spiritual freedom in Christ. Sin always tries to move in the opposite direction to what God desires. So our souls are not best equipped to lead us into freedom. They are designed to be the mechanisms that help us to live in *this* world (the natural world), but they were originally made to be in submission to the leading of the Spirit Who teaches us all things (John 14:25).

Jesus says in John 14:17 that the world cannot accept the Holy Spirit. The Greek word for "world" is *kosmos*, which means the physical creation and worldly affairs. So basically Jesus is saying the Holy Spirit has different ways of operating; different intents and purposes; and different goals in mind, than what our natural thinking is inclined to lean on.

Because of this, our souls just don't have the right tools to discern what the Spirit wants for us. These are things that must be revealed or taught to us. And this is the beginning of stepping into increased spiritual freedom in Christ. It's learning that our best thinking, or our most pure emotional responses, or the very best choices we make, *if they are self-dependent, will not lead us into experiencing increased freedom in Jesus.* Our souls must submit to the Spirit and be taught. We need to acknowledge that our natural self is not the source of our freedom, that must come from the Spirit who promises to teach us everything we need to learn to live free.

So, what do we do to step onto that path?

Here are five key principles that will help you on the pathway to experiencing increasing freedom in Jesus.

1. Humility

I kind of hate to admit it, but I can be a pretty prideful man. I don't really like it when I don't have answers or look like I don't have what it takes to succeed. When I feel like I'm not portraying an image of someone who has things in order or that I'm incapable on my own, then I can experience real frustration. I'd rather be that guy who never needs to pull over and ask for directions because he thinks he already knows where to go. But as I have already shared about my road trip with relatives, I don't always know the answers.

In the same way, my soul is just not designed to know the directions of how to get to that place of spiritual freedom because it just doesn't have the ability. I need to pull over and ask Jesus for help, but even before that I need to admit that I can't do it on my own.

I need to be humble.

Being humble and being humiliated can sometimes seem like next door neighbours. They live *very* close to each other. Jesus calls me to humility, and Satan tries to make it feel and look like humiliation. Jesus wants the Spirit to guide me into that place where I can be humble, and Satan wants my soul to rise up in pride and never admit weakness or need. Which one do you think leads toward spiritual freedom?

Proverbs 22:4 says, "Humility is the fear of the Lord; its wages are riches and honour and life." If we will show proper reverence, respect, and awe toward the Lord (fear), then we will recognize just how brilliantly He shines and how He is so much more powerful and willing to set us free.

Humility is saying, "I can't but you can."

2. Ask for help

Telling God that you don't have what it takes on your own to experience spiritual freedom is a great place to start, but it is only the first step. You need to go further. And going further means that you don't just acknowledge that you're stuck but that you actually ask for help.

I love how God encourages us on our quest for experiencing increased freedom in Him when He lays it out in plain language in Matthew 7:7–8 NLT.

"Keep on asking, and you will receive what you ask for. Keep on seeking, and you will find. Keep on knocking, and the door will be opened to you. For everyone who asks, receives. Everyone who seeks finds. And to everyone who knocks, the door will be opened"

I am reminded of a statement Wayne Gretzky said many years ago when someone asked him to share a thought about why he was so successful. He said part of his success was that he was fearless to shoot the puck and when pressed to explain why he said something like this: "You miss 100% of the shots you never take." You will never score if you don't take a shot.

There is something to be said about this philosophy of Gretzky's when it comes to experiencing increased spiritual freedom in our souls. You see, if we never challenge our thinking by considering the possibility that our minds need help from an outside source in order to experience freedom, we will never experience it. If you don't take a shot, you will miss 100% of the time.

If our emotions are so deeply entrenched in the world around them, then we will only find those familiar and oh-so unsatisfying feelings that leave us empty and frustrated. We may need to consider taking a different approach, a different path, a different way that challenges our feelings of safety and familiarity, because if we don't, we miss 100% of every shot we never take.

It may come down to choosing a very unfamiliar path. This may sound pretty tame, maybe even inviting on some level, until you begin to realize that we are talking about our very *lives*. What happens when we make a choice to follow Jesus and that means having our incomes reduced to such a degree that house payments can no longer be made? Choosing this path would likely feel like a devastatingly *wrong* choice was made. People around you might think you are very irresponsible and not providing a good witness to people about God. After all, Jesus came to bring *abundant life*, right? How is losing your house exemplifying abundance?

I'm not suggesting that choosing to be all-in for Jesus means that you will automatically suffer what I suggest above. But if we think that our value system is what dictates what Jesus should and shouldn't do, then we won't be in alignment with Him, and when that happens, our experience of spiritual freedom in Him suffers. Our lives are in *His* hands, and He cares for us, but we need to trust Him to teach us His ways which are sometimes in opposition to what we value.

So because our souls are still in a struggle with sin, we need to learn how to learn from the Holy Spirit who resides in our spirit. We need to be humble enough to ask Him for help, and we need to actually ask Him. Talk to Him. He loves it when we pray and listen. That is a good place to start, but there is more for us to do in order to live in increased spiritual freedom in Jesus.

3. Receive help

Have you ever been at a restaurant when it came time to pay the bill? You and your friend both went to the till, and once there you had the friendly war over who would pay? You want to, but your friend stands his ground and refuses to accept. It's such a strange dance: the whole thing is about wanting to bless each other, but somewhere along the way it morphs into a subtle stand-off. It gets even stranger if this is a close friend that you hang out with quite a bit which means that you have this bizarre scene play out a number of times as you do life together.

I can think of a friend who did this dance with me, and more often than not it ended with him paying the bill. Don't get me wrong, it was a very nice gesture, but after a while it made me feel as though he was unwilling to receive any blessing from me, and this had a slightly negative impact on our relationship. It seemed like there was a control issue buried in there somewhere, and it probably affected me too. But at the end of the day, it seemed to me that there would be an increase in the blessing of the relationship if there was a giving *and* a receiving that was taking place. I don't see this as a fairness thing, but more like a willingness to be open, vulnerable, and trusting... giving and receiving.

Receiving something from someone else expresses that you *value* what's being offered. Well, more than that actually. It's not primarily about valuing the gift being offered, but it's valuing the person that is offering it. To receive the gift is kind of like saying you receive the person who is giving it.

Who Jesus is and what He does for us is the perfect example of the importance of receiving. It was His love for us that drove Him to the cross. Love because He knew full well that sin had created an unbridgeable separation between people and God. His love moved Him to provide His own life as the bridge that would allow people to, once again, be connected to this God who loves. Jesus wanted that for each and every one of us.

But the interesting thing about this gift of salvation is that it's tied *directly* to Him! Yes, He died on the cross, but He also rose from the grave and lives, and so when we are invited to receive salvation from sin, we are actually being invited to receive *Him*.

We can't possess salvation unless we accept Jesus Himself as our gift of life.

This paradigm of receiving is very important for us to understand deeply, and the reason for this is because the life that *is* Jesus, that now resides within us in our newly revived spirit, still encounters distance from our souls. The gap between our holy identity in the Spirit and our still sin-wrestling soul is similar to what we experienced before we were in relationship with Jesus at all. There was distance and separation. And we already know that anything that is still immersed in sin has a really hard time accepting the things of the Spirit as we read in 1 Corinthians 2:14 that says, "But people who aren't spiritual can't receive these truths from God's Spirit. It all sounds foolish to them and they can't understand it."

We have the Holy Spirit of Jesus (Romans 8:9) living in us, and we have a soul that's still struggling to become holy through sanctification, which is an ever-increasing submission to the Spirit. But we still have times when we *think* the things of God don't really make sense. We still have times when we *feel* emotions that are not holy. And we still have times when we make *choices* that do not add up to holiness. There is still some *distance* between our souls and our spirits. But God is at work in us to overcome that distance, just like He was motivated to bridge the gap that sin had caused between people and God.

One of the keys to increasingly experiencing the freedom that already resides in our spirits is to *receive* it. To be willing to let go of worldly thinking, feeling, and choosing and to actually receive the gift of life and freedom. New thinking. New feelings. New choices. All the result of *receiving*.

But you are probably wondering how to do that? How do I receive the freedom that is residing in my spirit? How do I experience the life-changing power of the Holy Spirit in my soul?

Well, it's really no different than how you accepted Jesus in the first place.

The Spirit of Jesus has already been working on you, maybe even through this book, to see that there is another way to gain increased spiritual freedom in your life. This leads to a recognition of humble awareness. . there is a better way and something needs to change. This humility leads you to a place where you ask Jesus for help. This is stopping and asking Him to show you a pathway that would lead your soul into increased freedom. Once you ask Him, then you begin to realize that you are not really asking for a gift of freedom that is separate from Him, but that it's about entering into a new kind of relationship and experience *with* Him! Receiving freedom in your thinking means that you now enter into conversations about what you think about things in your life, and how you think about things in your life. You begin to invite Him into a dialogue, and you make a decision to ask, seek, and listen to what He has to say.

Maybe you've had trouble with anger, as an example, but you want that to change. So you begin to receive Him into your anger and allow Him opportunities to teach you why you respond the way you do, and invite Him to show you a different pathway to peace.

Or maybe you have a history of making choices that really put you in a bind in your life. Receiving Jesus into your will and beginning to talk and listen to Him will begin to shape the way you choose, the things you choose, and you will slowly become transformed into freedom.

At the beginning of this chapter I chose John 14:6–7 in which Jesus describes *Himself* as the way, truth, and life. This simply must not be underestimated for our journey into increased experience of the freedom that already resides in our spirit through Jesus. Jesus actually wants to teach our souls the way forward. He wants this because He loves us beyond our imagining. He desires that the truth of what He has already done in our spirit is something that He wants our souls to experience as well. He knows full well that it's in our souls that we live and are aware, and He wants them to be as free as our spirits. It's not just formulaic truth that He wants to teach us; it's truth that comes to us in the form of a person who *is* truth. Something amazing happens to us when Truth wraps His arms around us! Our defences go down, and we begin to lose our obstinate pride that always wants to pay the bill and has a really difficult time receiving the gift from someone else.

It's Jesus *Himself* in our spirit that is constantly inviting our souls to receive Him. When He shows us a way forward into freedom, and then He backs it up with truth and trustworthiness, He then allows the brilliance of His very *life* to become ours in our awareness. This is the goal and where true freedom resides... in the sharing of His life. The boundaries of my life and His life become blurry, lost in the brilliance of the Son Jesus, just like Paul experienced and describes in Philippians 1:21 when he says, "For to me, to live is Christ, and to die is gain." For Paul, life means Jesus. And when this chapter of his life is over, he considers the end a *gain* because then he would be face to face with Jesus forever!

We don't just receive Jesus once when we say "yes" to Him for salvation. If we live like that, then our souls will struggle for the entirety of our time on earth. Our experience of spiritual freedom will be greatly diminished. Instead, we're invited to say "yes" to Jesus again and again, in order for our souls to learn how to become increasingly spiritual and *free*. But that means humbly asking and receiving His life afresh in the daily grind.

4. Trust Him

I remember the imaginary and inspiring story of a man who made his living on the highwire. He came to a town that was built next to some deep canyons, and these filled him with not only inspiration for his show but also moved him to see these canyons as metaphors for the harsh valleys that come along in life.

He wanted the show in this town to be different, and so he began to plan how he would capture the imagination of the people and draw them to a place where they would begin to think about how their lives could find meaning.

He started by putting up posters around town that on a certain day the people should come to the canyon closest to town where they would experience a spectacle that would arrest and inspire them. And as the day approached, he meticulously planned his highwire act that would outshine any he had done before. He figured out how he would anchor his wire, organized all the gear he would need, and then finalized how he would put it all together.

The day finally arrived. He had his highwire firmly anchored on each side of the canyon and was confident in its integrity... it would hold his weight. He had thought through what he would say and what he would do, and was ready. Now he just needed to wait for everyone to arrive.

And arrive they did! This was not a town that was accustomed to a spectacle such as this, and the people were excited and intrigued to see exactly what this entertainer would do. And they wouldn't be disappointed!

Once they arrived they could see the anchors that had been driven into the rock and how they firmly held the highwire in place. They could see the entertainer in his garish costume but didn't look down on him because they just knew that the extreme nature of the act required extreme clothing to accompany it.

And then the time arrived. The crowd pressed in and the clownish looking man began to rise up and address the crowd. He told them how he would defy death this day by walking across the canyon on the impossibly thin wire. And then he would do so again by walking across while pushing a wheelbarrow! But the truly immense finale would come with a surprise that would cause the whole crowd to tremble at the magnitude of the invitation.

And so the entertainer walked across. He did so with flair, adding the oh-so-right amount of feigned stumbling that caused the people to gasp with fear and delight. And then he walked back again accomplishing the feat with such ease that the people were simply in awe.

And then he embarked a second time. But this trip had him pushing a wheelbarrow across in front of him! He explained that this simple gardening tool wasn't a challenge because of its weight as it was quite manageable. Instead, the life-threatening challenge was that it blocked his line of sight, so crossing meant he would have to somehow navigate it blindly trying to align the wheel with the wire. No easy task.

And the people could see that this new attempt to cross, while pushing this implement, was no simple or easy task. Where they could see before that the man traversing the chasm was a master who was faking the difficulty by providing a few well-planned missteps, now it was evident that he was truly taking his time in order to make it safely across.

But he did! And the whole crowd let out a collective sigh of relief when the feet of this courageous man moved from the suspended wire to solid ground on the other side. And then slowly, intently, and with great concentration, he stepped out one more time with the life-threatening barrow in front, and moved across to the side where the heart-skipping people watched with rapt attention.

They cheered him with a mixture of relief and amazement when he arrived at their side of the canyon. And then they quickly remembered that he had promised there would be *three* crossings and the last would far outshine the previous two. They wondered at what possibly could have been concocted in the mind of this man?

As was mentioned before, when the entertainer had first come to the town and saw the great canyon close by, it made him very introspective about his own journey in life. There had been many hard times where he struggled to survive, and he expended much energy to try and get ahead in his life. But though he had found a small amount of success, he could never overcome his lack of peace that caused him years of heartache. That is until he met Jesus. But he found it a struggle to entrust his life to this man who had accomplished another public spectacle that amazed the people that were gathered around him. His great show was to defeat sin on a cross by giving his life.

Somehow the entertainer knew that he needed to give his life to Jesus, and this required an act of trust. Many times this required him to actively put his life into the hands of his Saviour, and many times it required a new act of faith. This was the important message that he knew these town folks that surrounded him now needed to hear. And so he shared his heart with them. He told them about his life, his desires, his pride and success and his ever-present lack of peace that was only really addressed when he entrusted his life to Jesus who promised to carry him.

And then he turned to the crowd and said that trusting someone else with your life comes with very real-life implications. Trusting Jesus is like being invited to get into this wheelbarrow and trusting that I can take you across to the other side safely... .

And then he invited them to do just that. The man who had proven that he had what it takes to navigate the great divide, was now asking people to join in and experience it for themselves.

He invited and then waited, knowing that what he had just asked them had massive implications for their lives. He knew that the words that he spoke had just turned this whole show into something entirely different, and they needed some time to process it. After all, trusting someone with your life is no small thing.

So he waited. And waited. And waited some more. And then finally the most unassuming, kindly, and gentle person meekly stepped forward and said, "I will trust." The entertainer was overcome as he watched this man walk toward him with a childlike faith that had no hint of a person seeking the extreme adventure. He somehow sensed that this man had heard the invitation to entrust his life to One who could change it, and this was the means through which it would take place.

It made something rise up in the soul of the entertainer that strengthened him and caused an overwhelming thought: "I will not fail you!"

And so they took their first steps out onto the wire: the one who made the invitation and the one who said he would put his life into the hands of another. The crowd was watching in stunned silence as this unlikely duo crawled across the great divide. There were no missteps, There were no feigned close calls. The crossing had become very real, and everyone there could feel the apprehension in their bones. Not one single person made a sound. No one hardly even breathed. But all felt the electricity and intensity of life and death all around them.

The entertainer didn't fail. He brought his cargo home safely. The man in the wheelbarrow came back with something new... it was as if his countenance had become pure joy. It was not because of the adrenalin rush of crossing the canyon, but was instead his immersion into what a trusting faith in Jesus could bring: *freedom*!

Friends, this is what it's like to experience freedom in Jesus. It starts with a response to the call of God to receive His Son for salvation so that your spirit may be made alive and you can receive new life and become a brand new creation, made holy and fully immersed in your new identity. And though this is a massive first step of trust, it's still only the first. Once you've been given this incredible gift, you're then asked to trust Jesus with another call, one that's not directed to your spirit but to your soul. You are now being asked to trust Him with all the patterns of thinking that you have adopted over the years as you've tried to navigate all of life's challenges and victories. The deep ruts that help to make life make sense as you've experienced it, and that are always pulling you in ways that are affected by sin; ways often at odds with God's ways. This leads to bondage, and this is something the Lord wants to free you from so you will experience freedom, not just imagine it as some future gift to be received when we meet Jesus face to face. *But it requires getting in His wheelbarrow.*

Will you trust Him with your thinking? Will you trust Him with the ways that you have carved out your living and in some ways your *life* over the last number of years? Experiencing the fruit of the Spirit in your life only happens when your soul submits to Him and agrees to live in agreement with Him and His ways. Imagine how the man who was invited to step into the wheelbarrow felt? His best laid plans; his years of hard work and diligence; his intention and sacrifice; all were set aside in order to receive something that required him to give up control. This is how freedom arrives in your soul.

And it's worth it!

You may be feeling something as you read this. Do you sense apathy toward this idea of radical trust in Jesus? Do you feel a sense of irresponsibility at giving up the reigns of control in your life? Do you have a twinge of joy at the possibility that there is really something to this, something that's evident on the distant horizon of your soul's awareness but not big enough to command the full weight of your attention? This too is your soul reacting to the invitation coming from Jesus. It's your feelings that have been given to you as part of your image bearing of Him. And He wants full access to your feelings. He's not afraid of them. He's not intimidated by them. He's not disappointed in you because of your fear or pride or doubt or caution... He's wanting your feelings to be set free in Him so you will experience what it's like to live in this world apart from the bondages of what this world provides.

You may not be compelled by what I'm sharing here to the degree that you sense that you're being asked to make a decision, a decision to commit your soul... your ways of thinking and your ways of feeling, to Jesus afresh. But you need to understand that when the *idea* of living in a new freedom in Jesus is presented, it's meant to cause you to pause and consider it. These ideas lead to feelings that encourage or discourage courses of action, and that leads us to the third and final part of your soul... your will.

To experience increased freedom in Jesus requires an act of your will. It's not only based on your thoughts and feelings because you've been designed to take these first two things and *apply them toward action*. To make a choice for Jesus is never something to take lightly, and He knows this, and He walks with you with great care and sensitivity in order to make the path straight for you to choose Him over and against everything else.

Will you choose Him? Will you choose to submit your thoughts and ideas to Him? Will you choose to offer Him all your feelings and lay them down? It all boils down to a choice... and to choose this course of action is to open the doors of experiencing freedom that will pay beautiful and tangible dividends that were previously hidden to you.

Revelation 12 reveals the incredible battle between the evil plans of Satan and powerfully redeeming plans of God. In the middle of this titanic struggle are people just like you and I. These people were immersed into a conflict of epic proportions when Satan was thrown to earth and began his campaign of deception.

But in the midst of this carnage, the brothers and sisters of Jesus were given tools that are so powerful that when enlisted, they overwhelmed the power of the devil and set people free. It says in verse 11: "And they have defeated him by the blood of the Lamb and by their testimony" (NLT).

The blood of Jesus breaks the dominant power of the devil, and when people receive Jesus as their Saviour, He breaks the back of sin and brings people into new life and new identity as His brothers and sisters. The *word of testimony* is the ongoing invitation that is offered to the bride of Christ in order to release the power of the truth of God. We are called to testify according to the Word of God (Jesus) and the word of God (Bible) about who He is, and about who *we* are in Jesus.

Our soul's freedom depends on both of these things: The blood of Jesus and the word of our testimony. What an incredible invitation! To be invited to participate in the overcoming of the work of the devil in order to see freedom reign on this earth, *and in my life*! It just requires acting as Jesus did toward His heavenly Father. He submitted to the wisdom of God and His plan for salvation and life. He overcame his fears by continually offering them to God through prayer. He conquered death by choosing to walk the path that God desired for Him to walk.

In every way, the soul of Jesus was in alignment to the Spirit. And in the end life won.

This is your invitation as well. To apply the blood of Jesus to your soul's ways of thinking, ways of feeling and ways of choosing, by declaring in prayer to God your humble submission to Him so that He will apply His freedom to you.

Trusting Jesus will increase freedom in your soul.

5. Abiding in Jesus

Before I began to write this book, Jesus spoke to me in a time of prayer. I was in a place where I felt there were some significant decisions needed in order to follow the path that He had for me. I'd like to share some of the significant parts of that prayer with you because it has elements that will benefit you in your journey toward increased freedom in Jesus. Here's what the Lord told me:

> *Brian, I have heard your prayer, and I will speak to you. I have heard the cry of your heart, and I receive it as a holy cry. You have asked forgiveness for your many fears that have become idols in you. I forgive you Brian and wash you clean. What seems like an unbridgeable gap to you is nothing to Me. The discipline you desire, I am able to provide for you, but you must ABIDE in Me. Stop visiting Me and ABIDE in Me. I am your refuge but you need to pursue Me in order to experience the blessing of being found in Me. Brian you are clean. You don't feel it, I know, but that is not because you aren't clean, it's because you are not ABIDING in Me. You don't understand how and so I will teach you, but you still must pursue Me with all your heart, soul, mind, and strength. There are things coming up in your mind that you know you need to do, but you are still afraid that you will fail. I AM HERE WITH YOU MY SON. I WILL NEVER LEAVE YOU NOR FORSAKE YOU. I will be your strength; I will be our guide; I will be your teacher; I will be your peace. Brian, would you give your whole life to Me and trust Me with it? This IS what I'm asking of you; your whole life is Mine, give it to Me. I will purify your heart, Brian. I will stretch it out like a sail to catch the wind of My Spirit. I will show you things that you couldn't understand now even with your greatest efforts. But in order for you to receive all this, YOU MUST ABIDE IN ME. Seek Me and trust Me and I will give to you abundantly.*

One thing we have unfortunately learned in western culture is how we highly value education apart from transformation. If we want to make our way we need to learn what is needed in order to accomplish the task. Learning the skill doesn't require changed character in order to get the job done. Even though learning is good and is something that God has given us the capacity to do, the effects of sin on learning is that it takes on an objectivity that holds the knowledge at a distance from us as people. We have built a system of knowledge acquisition that does not require the transformation of our character in order to accomplish great things. We apply this same method when it comes to our walk with Jesus. We learn the right words and doctrines; principles and procedures, and apply them to situations in order to live what we see as right and good.

The problem we have is this: If we learn truth objectively and separately or outside of ourselves, and Jesus calls Himself the *Truth*, then we will treat Jesus objectively and separate from ourselves as well. *We can never experience deep and abiding freedom in our souls if we hold Jesus at a distance from our souls.*

And so *abiding* becomes incredibly important. Jesus wants us not to depend on our rational minds independently from Him. He wants us to invite Him into our minds so He can transform them from worldly influence. Jesus wants us not to navigate our feelings and reactions to things in our lives on our own, but instead wants us to intentionally offer each and every emotion to Him so that He can transform them to respond in fullness and freedom. Jesus isn't looking for us to exercise our wills apart from Him, but is instead inviting us to submit them to Him so that He can influence and shape them to be able make choices that arise from heaven's wisdom and not worldly wisdom.

Jesus is inviting us into a whole-life transformation that will require us to give up our road maps and entirely trust Him to chart a new path for us. And the only way we can receive this is to *abide* in Jesus.

Abiding means to do life with Him not for Him. It means recognizing that He does not get ticked off at us when we ask Him constantly for guidance for our thoughts, feelings and choices. Abiding means that we become *immersed into Him in daily life*. We don't take vacations from Him, but instead invite Him to come on vacation with us. Abiding in dependence on Him is strange because it flies in the face of what we have breathed in our culture since the day we took our first breath. But it's *exactly* what He wants for us. Did you pick up on that last sentence? I said, "it is exactly what He wants *for* us." He knows that if we will abide in Him, then we will receive. Do you know what it is that we will receive?

Freedom.

Final Thoughts

In my office I have a framed document from someone I have grown to really admire over the years. His name is Bill Johnson. I'm sure you've heard of the Bill Johnson of Bethel fame before, but you've probably not heard of *this* Bill Johnson. The man I'm talking about used to live near the small town of Strasbourg, Saskatchewan, and even though he has been gone for a few years, his influence still lingers through my memories and through his family who I hold in very high regard.

This is what Bill Johnson offered as sage wisdom for life:

> Don't have a fit.
> Seek the Lord.
> Find a way.
> Don't give up.

Blunt. Straightforward. To the point. And filled with wisdom.

When we experience life by trying to make our way independently from God, we will carry with us a lack of freedom that can weigh us down incredibly. And because life simply will never stop coming at us, we can feel overwhelmed which leads to "having a fit." It may not necessarily be visible to others (though it might be!), but the chaos within is just as real, and just as devastating.

Bill Johnson shares his wisdom with us by saying the best course of action is to seek the Lord. And He's right on the money. Our seeking needs to be so intentional and so consistent that it needs a special word to describe it and that word is *abiding*. We need to abide in Jesus. Do all of life with Him. He made us as brand new creations in our spirit through His gift of life, and is working overtime to reveal Himself anew in our souls so that we would become expressions of overwhelming freedom in this world. As we abide in Jesus, He shines through us so others can see Him. People will see our freedom, that flies in the face of life circumstances, which gives rise to desires in them to be free as well. The freedom of our souls matters a lot to Jesus!

If we commit to abiding in Jesus what we will discover through Him are ways of living that were previously hidden to us. Bill Johnson says that after we don't have a fit, and after we seek Jesus, we then need to find a way. Jesus *is* our way. He is the Truth, the Life and the Way. And He is not just *the* way, He is *our* way, waiting to be discovered.

I love the fact that God encourages us by telling us clearly that He is for us and not against us (Romans 8:31). He reminds us that His power is at work in us (Phil. 2:13). He teaches us that He is committed to finishing what He has started (Phil. 1:6). With all of this then we have been given what it takes to accomplish Bill Johnson's final encouragement and that is: Don't give up.

Jesus faced very hard challenges. He didn't give up, and because of His perseverance, freedom was offered to the whole world.

You face hard circumstances too. Don't give up because you have been made new in your spirit through the life of Jesus and are now being invited into a journey where your soul experiences freedom it never knew possible.

It's not a pipe dream; it's real. It's the heart of the Father for you. It's the passion of Jesus for you. It's the commitment of the Holy Spirit in you.

And I add my voice to cheer you on. With Jesus, you can step in and experience the freedom that has been won for you. His invitation stands, and His arms are open wide.

Take His hand and be blessed on your journey into a new land.

About the Author

BRIAN M. TYSDAL has fifteen years of experience as a pastor in urban and rural settings and has spent nine years leading an independent renewal ministry called Deeper Life. He has witnessed and walked through the struggles and joys that most of the disciples of Jesus encounter. During the past two years, he has had the opportunity to delve into what a deeper life in Jesus really looks like and how his identity is bound to Christ's. Throughout this process, his heart and mind were shaped to share his experiences. The result is *Know Yourself and Live Free*.

Brian is a first-time author. He lives in Strasbourg, Saskatchewan, Canada, with his wife, Val, of thirty-six years.

He is the founder and CEO of Deeper Life Ministries. DL is a renewal ministry focused on prayer and worship as the primary means of inviting people into transformative encounters with Jesus. If you want more information about Deeper Life Ministries go to www.deeperlifeministries.ca or contact Brian at brian@deeperlifeministries.ca.

Printed in Canada